Strategy by Design

Strategy by Design

A Process of Strategy Innovation

James Carlopio

The Library of Congress has cataloged the hardcover edition as follows:

Library of Congress Cataloging-in-Publication Data

Carlopio, James.
    Strategy by design : a process of strategy innovation / James Carlopio.
        p. cm.
    Includes bibliographical references and index.
    ISBN 978–0–230–62022–3
    1. Strategic planning. I. Title.

HD30.28.C3765 2010
658.4'012—dc22   2009025394

A catalogue record of the book is available from the British Library.

Design by Newgen Imaging Systems (P) Ltd., Chennai, India.

First PALGRAVE MACMILLAN paperback edition: February 2013

D 10 9 8 7 6 5 4 3 2

CONTENTS

PURPOSE STATEMENT

The purpose of this book is to help you and your organization make a profit and a positive difference in our world by integrating your thinking hearts and feeling minds.

ACKNOWLEDGMENTS

I am indebted to many people who helped me with this book. First and foremost is David Grant, a graphic artist. David arranged for and accompanied me on the initial round of interviews I did in Sydney, Australia, and spent countless hours discussing design with me. He is responsible for a good chunk of my early design-related education.

I am, of course, also indebted to the many designers who so generously gave of their time, experience, and wisdom during the interviews. Thank you Frank Tyneski and colleagues at the Industrial Designers Society of America (IDSA), for all of your help, information, and contacts. Thank you Jeffrey Crass and colleagues at the Design Centre Enmore, Sydney, Australia, for your time and help. Thank you Rolf Pauw for the introduction to the Frankfurt Fair (Messe Frankfurt) and the European designers I was able to interview as a result.

Thank you Troy, for the fantastic cover image and thank you Mustafa, for your help with the model.

Another person responsible for a significant portion of my early design-related education and experience is Deborah Kneeshaw, a graphic designer and an excellent design educator. Deborah and I together ran several executive programs on creative strategic thinking in 1995/1996. During these programs, I learned more about design and its application to strategy development than I can articulate.

I also acknowledge and thank Tim Kiessling, a "strategy colleague" and friend of mine at Bond University, who was always ready, willing, and able to discuss strategy development and to provide me with ideas and help. I thank Kenichi Omhae, Michael Harvey, Cynthia Fisher, and Ben Shaw for their time, comments, and valuable feedback. Thank you to the staff of the Bond University Library, for your professional service and for finding me the scores of books and articles I continually requested.

I wholeheartedly express my thanks to Karen Lewis, College of Design, University of Kentucky, for providing me with so many excellent examples of design process and output. Thank you Simon Rippingdale and Todd Packer, for your generosity and your willingness to let me use your excellent images.

Finally, thank you my loves Bronte, Cassy, and Morgan. Your love and support are the world to me.

James Carlopio
Bond University
Gold Coast, Australia
jcarlopi@bond.edu.au

FOREWORD

All too often, when a book is written, the author modifies his/her existing book and makes modifications "on the margin" to the book. Less frequently, a book is written from scratch! The reason for that is authors want to leverage materials that they have already written and to maintain some modicum of the status quo in their chosen field (e.g., the author does not want to be too far in front of their field for fear of being branded a rebel or even in some cases a heretic). Not so for James Carlopio and his new book: *Strategy by Design: A Process of Strategy Innovation.*

Is a Radical Approach to Strategy Warranted?

The field of business has never seen change like it has in the last several years. The rate and amount of change has been unprecedented in the annuals of business history. Changes such as: (1) the increased number of regional integrated trading blocs (e.g., European Union, North American Free Trade Association, and twenty-one other such groups around the globe); (2) the growing importance of emerging markets (e.g., China, India, Argentina, Brazil, Mexico, and the like) holding seven-eighths of the future consumers of the world; (3) the growing importance of transitional economies after the "fall of the Berlin Wall"; (4) the ubiquity of technology throughout the world and the declining costs in computation, transportation, communication, and technology in general; (5) the liberalization of trade regulations stimulating global mobility of capital, products, and people; (6) the growing importance of knowledge-intensive economies and the resulting advent of the global e-commerce; and (7) the emergence of hypercompetition (e.g., increased importance of developing strategies using time as the basis for competitive strategies that "disrupt" the marketplace by generating creative/innovative competitive advantage based upon the global management's ability to generate new creative ideas and strategies).

The most significant change of all is the globalization of business. Our worldwide system of contemporaneously influential events, options, and constraints requires global managers to develop a systemic, innovative, and most importantly a creative approach to problems that have not been addressed in the past (e.g., a new model or paradigm shift in thinking for global managers). One has to ask if a "dusted off" version of a book that has been around for years and revised on the margins can address this magnitude of change. Will global managers gain the insights necessary to address the rate and amount of change taking place in the marketplace? One comes to the conclusion fairly rapidly—that a revised approach to the past problems of business is not what is needed. An innovative approach to the brave new world of global business is indeed a requirement for training a new breed of global managers.

One needs to question and suspend their knowledge built upon experiences in business to date. Unlearning (e.g., reducing dependence on the conventional wisdoms derived from experience in the past) is clearly the hallmark of this book. The *art and science* of seeing and designing to generate different views and to develop innovative strategies given the changes taking place in the global environment of business is the goal of this book. The syllabus for learning to manage in the global marketplace is to clearly delineate the problem/goal, research the new global competitive environment for the conventional wisdoms of the future, concept generation (i.e., ideation), rapid prototyping (evaluation and redesign), and implementation, rapidly always recognizing the caveat that change will need to be quick and continuous if you want to be a long-term, successful global player.

Dr. Michael Harvey
Distinguished Chair of Global Business
University of Mississippi and Bond University (Australia)

CHAPTER ONE

Strategy by Design: A Process of Strategy Innovation

Organizational strategy is typically conceived and developed as an extension of the past and present. We analyze the market, the competition, the industry, and our internal resources and capabilities. We then reposition ourselves in existing markets or we extend our product/ services into developing or adjacent markets. The future is assumed to be a linear extension of the past and present, and our rational analytical techniques help us to do this well. What happens, however, when the future is not a linear extension of the past and present? What happens when we want to innovate and reinvent our business model, our industry, or our world? How can we radically add value and provide high quality at low cost? How can we reinvent the ailing automobile industry or the air-travel experience? How can we solve the problems of our broken health care system, our dysfunctional economy, or address global warming, hunger, poverty, and terrorism? Rational analyses of our internal and external environments will not help us create a future that is radically different from our past. Reinventing our business model, our industry, or our world requires strategy innovation, not just doing what we did last year plus 10 percent (i.e., 10 percent more, better, or less expensively).

The billion-dollar strategic questions are, therefore, "How do we generate strategy innovations? How do we make a profit and reinvent our organization, our industry, and our world?" Unfortunately, although millions of words and thousands of books and articles have been written on organizational strategy, there is little that can be used to help us create strategy innovations. In fact, Gary Hamel (1997, 1998) one of the world's most influential business thinkers according to *The Wall Street Journal*, said the dirty little secret of the strategy industry is that it does not have a theory of strategy creation and does not know where bold, new value-creating strategies come from. As hard as it is to believe, Hamel is right. More than ten years later the strategy industry still has no widely accepted theory, methods, or tools for the creation of strategy innovations. If these assertions—that (1) strategy development is traditionally conceived and developed as an analytical extension of the recent past and present into the future, and (2) that there are no clearly articulated theories or processes for the creation of strategy innovation—are correct, and since thousands of people in organizations worldwide continue to formulate strategy every year or so, one would expect the strategies that are developed to be less than successful and/or to be simply variants, or extensions, of what has been done in the past. This is, in fact, what the data suggest.

The data related to strategy success or failure overwhelmingly illustrate that mergers and acquisitions (Ashkenas and Francis, 2000; Freeman, 2005; Jonk and Ungerath, 2006; Lebihan, 2004), strategic restructuring and business process reengineering efforts (Cao, Clarke and Lehaney, 2001; Tai and Huang, 2007) as well as strategic repositioning initiatives (Raps, 2004; Turner and Crawford, 1998; Verweire, 2004) all consistently fail 50–80 percent of the time. The data also suggest when new strategies are implemented, they are usually simple variants or extensions of what has been done in the past. For example, Kim and Mauborgne (2004) studied organizations in over thirty industries examining data stretching back over one hundred years and found that 86 percent of new strategic ventures were line extensions (i.e., incremental improvements to existing industry offerings), while only 14 percent were aimed at creating new markets or industries. Similarly, McGahan (2004) found that between 1980 and 1999 only 6 percent of the strategic change trajectories among U.S. industries were creative change and 16 percent were radical (i.e., everything is up in the air), while most were either incremental (43 percent) or intermediating (32 percent) change (i.e., changes to the relationships of buyers, suppliers, and sellers typically the result of changes to information access). While incremental continuous improvements are important as line extensions and adjustments are necessary to stay competitive in our ever-changing world (e.g., to keep quality high, to keep profits from eroding, and to keep market share), we can only drive downsizing, cost reductions, and efficiency so far. In order to generate significant new wealth, we must create new sustainable competitive strategies, new business models, and new work processes. We must radically reinvent ourselves, our organizations, our industries, and many of our social institutions because real value and wealth creation goes to those who can innovate and redesign themselves and their industries. When we want a future that is no longer a linear extension of the past and present, we need strategy innovation.

While this is easy to say, and we know from a few often-touted cases (e.g., Cirque du Soleil and Apple Computers) that it can be done, what is not clear is how to do it. Several authors have provided advice, however. For example, according to Kim and Mauborgne (2004), the keys to developing radical "blue ocean" strategy innovations are to look for ways to find uncontested market space; ways to make the competition irrelevant; ways to create and capture new demand; ways to break the value/cost trade-off and "align the whole system of a company's activities in pursuit of differentiation and low-cost" (p. 81). According to Hamel's (1997) advice, the answer is to "unleash the spirit of strategy innovation...the ability to reinvent the basis of competition within existing industries and to invent entirely new industries. It will be the next fundamental competitive advantage for companies around the world. In an increasingly nonlinear world, only nonlinear strategies will create substantial new wealth." Unfortunately, while inspirational, these authors leave us with questions such as, "OK in theory, but how do I actually do that in practice? How do we create strategy innovations and find these uncontested, radical, nonlinear, innovative breakthrough strategies, business models, industries, and solutions?" The logical place to look is to the literature on strategy formulation and development.

Traditional Strategy Development

While there is no one widely accepted theory or process of strategy creation, there are many views of the strategy development process that have been identified and discussed. Mintzberg and colleagues (Mintzberg, Ahlstrand, and Lampel, 1998; Mintzberg and Lampel, 1999) discussed ten predominant schools of strategy formation (design, planning, positioning, entrepreneurial, cognitive, learning, power, cultural, environmental, and configuration). The first school of thought is referred to as the design school. One might expect that people who adhere to this design school actually would discuss the process of designing or creating strategy. However, in the design school the term "design" is used in its noun form, in the sense of a form or a structure, rather than in its verb form, in the sense of creating or generating strategy. The design school of strategy development does not tell us how to design strategy or where bold, new value-creating strategies come from.

The most well-known school of strategic thought is the positioning school popularized by Porter (1980). In this view, generating strategy is conceived as an analytical process of assessing the external environment (e.g., via Porter's five competitive forces) and discovering which of the three generic strategic positions (i.e., overall cost leadership, differenti-ation, or focus), or their variants or combinations, is likely to yield the highest return on investment. There is no discussion of how we create strategy.

As described by Mintzberg and colleagues, in the planning school, strategy is formally planned using a linear mechanistic process; in the entrepreneurial school, strategy is metaphorically envisioned in the mind of the entrepreneur; and in the cognitive school, it is constructed in senior managers' minds. In all three cases strategy is assumed to be formulated via environmental analysis, and then implemented with incremental adjustments to new or existing products/services and mar-kets. In the learning school, strategy emerges based on incremental trials and experiments; in the power school, strategy is negotiated, or power and persuasion are used to influence which strategies are cho-sen, but little is said about how strategy is generated in the first place; in the cultural school, strategy is formulated via an indistinct collective social process rooted in organizational culture; in the environmental school, strategy is said to be a reaction to the contingencies in the external environment; and finally, in the configuration school, pro-ponents are concerned less with strategy formulation per se than with how an organization transforms itself and changes states when strategy changes (Mintzberg and Lampel, 1999). All of these schools of strate-gic thought equate strategy formulation with analyses of the present and recent past extrapolated into the future. None of these schools of strategic thought provide models of, or processes for, the generation or creation of strategy innovation.

I examined the content of over forty texts on strategy formulation, strategy development, strategic management, strategic thinking, and the like looking to see if they articulated a process for strategy crea-tion. The most widely covered topic in the books, related to strategy formulation or strategy development, was external environmental analysis (covered in 76 percent of them). The next most widely cov-ered topics were the resource-based view of strategy and strategic capability/competency analysis (57 percent), corporate strategy (e.g., growth, M&A/takeovers, diversification; 55 percent), and Porter's five forces (52 percent). The importance of establishing a vision or mission came next (48 percent) along with Porter's three generic positions (i.e., low-cost, differentiation, and focus; 45 percent). Smaller numbers of texts covered issues such as scenario development and analysis (36 percent), the value chain (36 percent), and product portfolio/lifecycle analysis (33 percent). Few texts addressed the topics of emergent strategy (26 percent), incrementalism or logical incrementalism (17 percent), multiple views of strategy development (e.g., Mintzberg's ten views; 10 percent), or the importance of collaboratively developing strategy (5 percent). Only one text out of the forty-two I examined, *Strategy Making* by Eden and Ackerman (1998), was future-oriented, discussed strategy creation and creativity, and the need to iteratively develop strategy, as well as the importance of playfulness and fun. They even have a picture of Frank Lloyd Wright's residential masterpiece, Fallingwater, built near Pittsburgh, PA, on the book cover and so, I assume, saw the connection between architectural design as a process (design in its verb form) and strategy creation. Therefore, according to the vast majority of strategy development texts, the way to formulate strategy is to do extensive analyses of the external and internal environments, set your mission and vision, then position your organization in relation to those findings, create some scenarios to capture the outcomes, and incrementally adjust your existing strategy accordingly.

Consider the quintessential strategy development process-model from Rea and Kerzner (1997; see figure 1.1). Granted, the text may be considered old, but it perfectly exemplifies the majority of what is discussed in the strategy texts I examined. As we can see, the process starts with analyses of the internal and external environments. Once gathered (step 1), the information is evaluated (step 2) and somewhere between steps 2 and 3, some strategies are somehow formulated, so they can be evaluated (step 3), selected (step 4), and then implemented (step 5). The strategic options formulated, as we have seen, are most often incremental improvements to existing industry offerings. The texts are illustrative of the mainstream strategy development industry. They tell us what to do, based on analyses of what others have done in the past and are doing in the present, but not how to actually create strategy ourselves nor how to do it innovatively. That is why so much of the strategy we see developed is simply what we did "last year plus 10 percent."

Strategy by Design

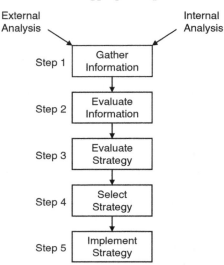

Figure 1.1   The traditional strategic planning model. Adapted from Rea and Kerzner (1997).

Design or Die: The Value of Design

Since the academic strategy literature, and strategy development and formulation textbooks, do not give us any answers, where else can we look? The design profession is well established in theory, research, and practice (cf. Archer, 1979; Davis et al., 2009; Haskell, 1940; Michlewski, 2008; Page, 1963; Seldes, 1932; Schutte, 1975; Sowrey, 1987; Taylor, 1969). Architects, industrial designers, graphic artists, and many others in the design professions have tried and tested processes for creating innovative structures, products, services, and solutions to problems. If we look to the well-developed and researched field of design, we can learn from them, and apply their processes to the design of strategy innovation. I am suggesting that we need to think in terms of using design theory and processes for the creation of strategy innovation, for the radical redesign of industries, and for the design of solutions to some of our most pressing large-scale social and global problems.

There is good evidence suggesting that steady investment in, and commitment to, design is rewarded by lasting organizational competitiveness (cf. Lester, Piore, and Malek, 1998; Michlewski, 2008; Nussbaum, 2004). Design's profile has been rising in the business world as people increasingly recognize its role in helping differentiate products and services in the global marketplace as quality becomes commoditized. As managers revise their view of design as cosmetic decoration and aesthetic afterthought, design may be seen as the last remaining competitive differentiator (Stevens, Moultrie, and Crilly, 2008). Evidence of this comes from the results of a Design Council (2006) study of the share prices of U.K.-based companies over the previous ten years. Their research found that a group of companies recognized as effective users of design outperformed key FTSE indices by 200 percent. The sixty-three companies, grouped into a Design Portfolio on the basis of their high level of success in numerous design award schemes, did substantially better than their peers in both the bull and bear markets between 1994 and 2003, the period covered by the study.

Further evidence of the value of design comes from many examples of organizations using design processes and thinking to generate strategy innovations and new business models successfully. For example, an agro-chemicals firm used design principles and process to radically change its strategy and value proposition from focusing on trying to sell sacks of herbicide to offering weed-free fields.

> From the customer's perspective, weed-free fields are what it is all about and how that is achieved is of less concern. The result of this experiment is that the use of agro-chemicals plummeted by 70 per cent as it was in the interests of the firm to use them efficiently rather than to sell as much as they could. And in shifting mindset from "we sell weed killers" to "we sell weed-free fields," they are free to explore alternative and more environmentally benign approaches. (Bruce, 2002, p. 264)

This is a radical strategy innovation that has the potential to transform the industry, adds significant value for the customer and the company, and helps address a critical environmental issue at the same time. A great example of strategy by design.

Another example comes from the Otis Elevator Company. According to Godin (2001), the basic problem with elevators is that they have to stop many times. While this certainly makes for frustrated users it is also a huge problem for building owners and designers.

> While your elevator is busy stopping at every floor, the folks in the lobby are getting more and more frustrated. The building needs more elevators, but there is no money to buy them and no where to put them. Otis's insight? When you approach the elevators, you

key in your floor on a centralized control panel. In return, the panel tells you which elevator will take you to your floor. With this simple pre-sort, Otis has managed to turn every elevator into an express... This means that buildings can be taller, they need fewer elevators for a given number of people, the waits are shorter, and the building can use precious space for people, not for elevators. A huge win, implemented at remarkably low cost. (p. 25)

Once again, this innovative system redesign provided significant benefits to all stakeholders.

A final related pair of examples that illustrate how we can design radical strategy innovations that transform an industry, add significant value for the customer and the company, and help address a critical environmental issue as well, starts with the Indego project, AT Kearney's reinvention of the automobile industry (Dunne and Young, 2004). They asked the following timely questions: If you could reinvent the automobile industry without any existing constraints, what would it look like? How could we change the industry and create significant value?

Old system: The initial car sales generate a profit for auto-makers (minimal profit given a mature industry with overcapacity and tough competition) and some opportunity to finance and provide spare parts. All other ongoing benefits and money-making opportunities go to others down-stream (e.g., sales dealers, service mechanics, and tire and muffler specialists).

New system: Auto-makers retain asset ownership and lease to consumers capturing all lifetime opportunities (e.g., maintenance, parts, onboard vehicle telemetry allowing traffic alerts, navigation advice, roadside assistance, and music/video downloads). The auto-makers are responsible for sustainable disposal of vehicles.

In a vein similar to the Indego project, Merloni Elettrodomestici, the European whitegoods manufacturer, redesigned its industry (Marsh, 2001; www.merloni.com accessed May 2009). As with the auto industry, margins are tight, the whitegoods industry is mature, and there is little room for competitors to move. Merloni had to adopt a defender strategy (Miles and Snow, 1984) to survive, cutting costs and focusing on production efficiencies. Instead of consumers' buying a washing machine, in the redesigned pay-as-you-wash industry model, the user pays a flat fee (e.g., 50 Euros) for a washing machine, plus a yearly leasing/service fee (approximately 300 Euros, the exact payment depends on usage). As well as the leasing initiative, Merloni is investing in service centers that handle calls about faulty appliances as well as fitting some machines with smart adapters that can automatically contact remote service sites via the Internet when the machine develops a problem.

In both of these cases, instead of having to continually play a loosing game of forever defending shrinking margins and market-share, they challenged and then redesigned the rules and added significant value for the consumer (e.g., smaller initial cash outlay, maintenance becomes easier, no responsibility for car/machine disposal), for themselves (e.g., they get increased margins, a new ongoing income stream, and opportunities for services and enhancements), and for the society (e.g., the producers remain responsible for the car/machine motivating them to recycle and properly dispose of it). Strategy by design wins again.

Strategy Innovation by Design

In order to use design to develop these types of radical strategy innovations and new business models, to help us redesign and reinvent our ailing industries, and to help us address some of our worst large-scale social and environmental problems, we must understand the design process and how it can be applied to the creation of strategy innovations and the design of solutions to large-scale, systemic problems. Toward this end, we will discuss the design process, and a model of it, synthesized from information gathered from interviews with design professionals[1] and from the vast professional and academic design literature.[2] This model will then provide the structure for the remainder of this book.

Design is not a linear process wherein we start with an idea, follow the five steps, and wind up with a successful product/service or solution. Unanimously, design is conceived as a dynamic process involving many iterations of increasingly interlinked feedback and feed-forward loops, with multiple inputs generating an emerging end result (cf. Blyth and Worthington, 2001; Cross, 1982, 2000; Summers, 2002; Vedin, 2005; Weick, 2004). In other words, design is not a linear task; it is a dynamic iterative process. While, in practice, the design process has a start and an end, once the process begins, it requires a three-dimensional mode of thinking. The two-dimensional world of linear thinking, numerical analysis, and rational problem-solving wherein we logically move from start to finish in a straight line, is not the world of the designer. Designers engage in a nonlinear, iterative dance, constantly balancing opportunities with anticipated problems, creativity with restrictions, conception with perception, and possibilities with budgets and deadlines.

Brown (2005) stated that design is "a process of enlightened trial and error in which we observe the world around us, identify patterns, generate ideas, get feedback, repeat the process, and keep refining until we are ready" (p. 54). In other words, the design process takes into account the fact that "Nothing is invented and perfected at the same time" (translated from a Latin proverb by Dodgson, Gann, and Salter, 2005). *Serious play*, a term coined by Schrage (2000), and the schema of *think, play, do* proposed by Dodgson, Gann and Salter (2005) best capture the spirit of the design process wherein we invent, test, develop, and redevelop our ideas via an iterative process involving the definition of a brief and identification of a problem, research into both the users'/ customers' and organization's requirements, prototyping or modeling several partial or potential solutions, and refining them via multiple feedback loops. Identifying problems, creatively thinking about and generating many potential solutions, and developing, testing, and evaluating those solutions is what designers do, and that is what strategists must do if they want to surprise and delight their customers, reinvent their industries and business models, and address our most pressing global issues. Prototyping, iterations, feedback, and a sense of discovery, creativity, and play are consistently stressed in discussions of the design process, and these aspects are sorely lacking in traditional discussions and models of the development of organization strategy.

The Value of a Process Model of Strategy Innovation by Design

Designing innovative strategies may seem risky at first. Incremental improvements to, and extension of, existing strategies, services, and products undoubtedly seem much safer than developing a completely new idea that challenges the status quo. As with all investments, however, higher risk has the potential to yield higher rewards, and sometimes, while trying something new is uncertain, staying with the status quo is certainly doomed to failure.

When we invest in new ventures, we try to mitigate the risk by balancing our portfolios of actions or choices and by planning for potential problems. This is one of the reasons why having a design process model is valuable. According to Bruce and Bessant (2002), "the value of a process model is that it provides milestones along the journey where these risks can be assessed" (p. 40).

> You can use it [a design process model] to educate the client. It helps make me efficient with my time. It helps get the project going and gets clients to make decisions. (Joel, Graphic and Communications Designer)

Not only do process models provide us with a series of decision-points at which we can assess progress and make decisions about changes in, or the continuation of the project, models also can serve as a guide ensuring repeatability of the process, and they provide a checklist of issues helping ensure that we do not leave out any essential steps of the process.

A Model of Strategy Innovation by Design

The vast majority of authors and designers agree that in the early stages of the design process a large amount of information must be collected from many sources. This information is first formed into a goal, problem, or brief (chapter two). The next step in the process is to conduct various forms of research (chapter three) to explore the problem, collect information that will help us generate ideas, and gain insights into the users/consumers, the competition, the organization, the market, relevant government policy, and so on. It is critical that both user issues (i.e., design issues related to the way the final designed outcome interacts with users of it) and maker issues (i.e., design issues related to realizing the outcome being designed—to do with production techniques, tools, materials as well as broader organization and industry analysis) must be considered (Boyle, 2004; Holt, 1990; Kimbell, Stables, and Green, 1996). Once we know what the brief is, and we have gained some insights into the users/consumers, the organization, and its internal and external environments, we use this information to help start the creative process of concept generation or ideation (chapter four). This creative, divergent thinking process is followed by the quick development of rough plans, models, or prototypes (chapter five). The divergent, expanding, creative impetus must be counterbalanced by a more convergent, inward, and practical thrust. This phase is indispensable to any creative project (Osborn, 1953). We must verify not only our final findings, but also intermediate stages, so we can focus on objectives and identify and challenge our assumptions. In other words, we must continually check back with the brief, evaluate the solution, adjust our efforts, and continue the process. This evaluation and refinement process is critical as it introduces accountability and safeguards into the design process. This convergent evaluation (chapter six) aspect allows the start of an iterative process of evolution, refinement, and redevelopment wherein we prototype/model, evaluate, and judge the results, refine solutions, check if they work and address the brief or solve the problem, creatively generate more ideas and/or modifications, and iterate/remodel until we are satisfied with the result or run out of time. According to many authors and designers, this iterative process of creative, divergent generation and convergent refinement is a key part of designing. Finally, we move to the stage where we make a decision and deliver or transfer the project output (chapter seven).

The overall process as discussed can be illustrated as in figure 1.2.[3] Some of the differences between the traditional strategy development process and the strategy by design process are highlighted in table 1.1.

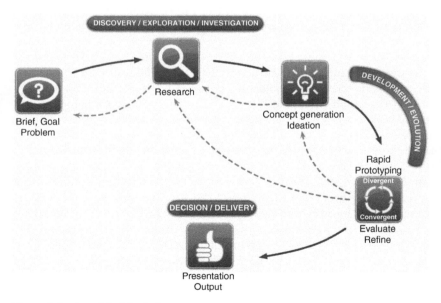

Figure 1.2   A model of the design process.

Table 1.1   Comparison of traditional strategy development and strategy by design

The process	Traditional strategy development	Strategy by design
The brief	Develop a winning strategy	Specification of requirements and constraints; clarification of and questioning of the problem, aims, and objectives of the project, assumptions, priorities, business and financial objectives, the project plan, and resource requirements and allocation; and establishment of performance targets and measures
Research	Hypothesis confirmation and decision justification; convergent and problem-focused; quantitative data collection and analysis; direct observation; identify facts	Discovery and exploration; divergent and solution focused; qualitative and quantitative data collection and exploration; participant observation; explore latent needs and possibilities
Concept generation	Focus on choosing the one best idea; rational, linear/vertical thinking	Generate many ideas; intuitive, creative/lateral thinking
Prototype	Not usually a part of the process	Prototype; iterate with multiple feedback loops; converge over time
Develop and evaluate	The answer or solution is rationally chosen, justified, or proven	The answer is developed and evolves over time; it is evaluated via both objective and subjective criteria
Output	Usually verbal or written	Routinely visual may be supplemented verbally and in writing

It is important to remember that this is a two-dimensional model of a nonlinear, three-dimensional, and intensely iterative process. In reality all the phases are overlapping and interlinked. The outputs of one stage are used repeatedly within a stage (e.g., the iterative development and evolution cycle) and as inputs to other stages. Several concepts or elements within the steps are repeated with different emphases at different times in the process. For example, prototyping is done to explore and generate ideas near the middle of the design process and again to help evaluate and then communicate or sell the idea at the end of the process. Research is done at the start for exploration and idea generation, and later on for evaluation. Participation and customer/employee involvement is another example. Designers suggest broad involvement in the process is critical at the start when establishing the brief, then during ideation and concept generation, and again later in the process during evaluation and testing. This overlapping and iteration may seem unusual and sloppy at first to many of us who are more linear thinkers and are trained in traditional "waterfall" processes where one step logically follows from the next discrete set of activities once completed, as in the rational decision-making model (e.g., 1. identify the problem, 2. identify decision criteria, 3. allocate weights to criteria, 4. develop alternatives, 5. analyze alternatives, 6. select alternative, 7. implement chosen alternative). This, however, is the value and elegance of the design process. It allows us to learn as we go and not have to have one set of answers and processes perfected before we move on to the next. It gives us freedom and scope to explore and creatively generate novel ideas and solutions. It enables us to move quickly between problem definition and solution, and to iterate between them until we find something that works. (See appendix for an integrated example of this entire process.)

CHAPTER TWO

The Brief: Begin with the End in Mind

Design does not begin as a personal expression, as art often does (Boyle, 2004). It begins with the formulation of a problem or a brief. The designers interviewed almost unanimously agreed:

> It's the most important thing. The brief and the site are what you have so that's a starting point and from there it always develops. (Connie, Architect)

> You need to be well informed at the start, what are the parameters? Some parameters are given to you and are special to a particular case while others are common across all...get all the information you can from the brief especially about the budget and any environmental issues. (Eberto, Architect)

> You have to extract the brief—you never get enough information. (Joel, Graphic and Communications Designer)

> We begin with a content development brief that goes to the committee for approval...Once we have the brief we can start the design. (Brad, Museum Design Manager)

> You need a brief. There's no doubt about it. What we like to do at the start of every project is have the client write it down. (Julia, Graphic Designer)

> As an architect I talk to the clients about what they want and I look at the words between the lines. I look between the requirements and the context for the need or I look for something special or a chance comment they make that leads me into relationship with them. (Chris, Architect)

The first step in the design process is to synchronize the designers thinking and the user's or client's thinking for a shared mental
model. (Filippo, Product and Process Designer)

In the traditional strategy development process the brief is assumed to
be something like "develop a winning strategy." Issues such as strategic intent and the organization's mission, vision, values, goals, and
objectives are also part of the brief for traditional strategy developers.
For designers, these are necessary but not sufficient elements of the
brief.

According to the design literature, elements of a clear brief include
identification of the users/customers, a clarification of the problem, the
mission, aims, and objectives of the project, identification and questioning of assumptions, priorities, business and financial objectives,
the project plan and resources, and an outline of performance targets
and measures (Blyth and Worthington, 2001; Boyle, 2004; Thackara,
1997). Also, a project management and reporting structure must be
decided upon (e.g., deciding who leads and when), and the change
control mechanism, signoff gateways (i.e., entry or exit points), an
appropriate client contact, and the design team and team structure must
be clarified.

According to Blyth and Worthington (2001), "Often, briefing is
taken as a short meeting at which someone is given an instruction (the
brief) and a bit of background on a project and asked to deliver a solution" (p. 3). In contrast, they suggested briefing should be thought of
as "an evolutionary process of understanding an organization's needs
and resources, and matching these to its objectives and its mission. It is
about problem formulation and problem-solving. It is also about managing change. Ideas evolve, are analyzed, tested and gradually refined
into specific sets of requirements." The process of establishing the brief,
therefore, is itself seen as an iterative process wherein we collect relevant information, and also analyze and question the initial definition of
the problem and the objectives of the project. In the remainder of this
chapter, therefore, we will discuss these and other related issues.

The Six Elements of the Brief

Hock (1999) and Weick (2004) proposed six elements or perspectives of
design activity that provide an excellent framework for a discussion of
the briefing process according to designers. Design activity starts with

an intense search for purpose (element 1), and then moves on to principles (element 2), people (element 3), and concept (element 4), followed by identification of appropriate structure (element 5) and practices (element 6). These six elements are interrelated and overlapping. Each element can be thought of as a perspective or a lens (Hock, 1999, p. 7) through which we can examine design, the brief, and their application to the development of strategy innovation. Within this framework we will discuss some of the many issues that should be considered as part of the brief at the outset of the strategy innovation creation process and then regularly reviewed and updated as the project progresses.[1]

Purpose: A Binding Intent Worthy of Pursuit

There are three important components to this first element of establishing a purpose that provides a binding intent worthy of pursuit that must be considered at the start of the briefing process: (1) defining the purpose of the project or problem to be solved, (2) the purpose must supply a binding intent providing coherence and motivation, and (3) the purpose of the activity must be considered worthy of pursuit.

Defining the Purpose

We cannot start working to solve a problem until we have agreement on what the problem is. One of the important functions of the brief, therefore, is to establish a shared understanding of the problem, and the project goals and objectives, addressing questions such as: What is it we are trying to do and why? What do we hope to achieve? What are our aims, goals, or objectives? What are our deliverables, essential requirements, constraints (e.g., budgets and timeframes), and so on? According to Bernstein (1988) the brief plays an important role as a tool, an ally, and a partner in the journey toward a solution because the solution is likely found within the framing of the problem.

The Problem of Problem Definition

While it may sound easy to define the purpose of a design or strategy innovation project, we have known for many years that one of the most difficult problems we face is that of defining our problems in the first place (cf. Grint, 2005; Lyles, 1987). Consider Rittel and Webber (1973) who, while discussing the wicked problems inherent in the planning process, stated that "By now we are all beginning to realize that one of the most intractable problems is that of defining problems" (p. 159). In other words, the statement of the problem often is the problem. Cougar (1996) and Cross (2000) also discussed the difficulty and importance of defining problems and suggested that design problems are often initially vague and ill-defined, so that part of the task of finding a solution is to properly formulate the problem in the first place. According to Archer (1979):

> It is widely accepted...that design problems are characterized by being ill-defined. An ill-defined problem is one in which the requirements, as given, do not contain sufficient information to enable the designer to arrive at a means of meeting those requirements simply by transforming, reducing, optimizing or superimposing the given information alone. Some of the necessary further information may be discoverable simply by searching for it, some may be generateable by experiment...and some may be actually unknowable. In addition, once known, some of the requirements may turn out to be incompatible with one another. As it happens, most of the problems that most people face most of the time in everyday life are ill-defined problems in these terms. Not surprisingly, in the course of evolution, human beings have found quite effective ways of dealing with them. It is these ways of behaving, deeply rooted in human nature, that lie behind design methods. (p. 17)

The same is often true for strategy problems: "We need to find an extra two million dollars to rip out in costs"; "We need to make our product/service more appealing to customers while maintaining revenue margins"; "How can we generate an additional ten million dollars in revenue next year?"; "How can our group comply with existing regulations and expand our services while adding value using only existing resources?"; "We need to increase sales by 20 percent"; or "We have to stop our competition from continuing to win market share from us." These are certainly vague and ill-defined at the start. If we take the first part of the quote from Archer (1979) given earlier and reword it, it sounds just as "right" for strategy:

> It is widely accepted that strategy problems are characterized by being ill-defined in which the requirements, as given, do not contain sufficient information to enable the strategist to arrive at a means of meeting those requirements simply by transforming, reducing, optimizing or superimposing the given information alone. Some of the necessary further information may be

discoverable simply by searching for it, some may be generateable by experiment and some may be actually unknowable. In addition, once known, some of the requirements may turn out to be incompatible with one another.

This highlights the difficulty and importance of defining strategy problems and illustrates that strategy problems are often "wicked" (cf. Camillus, 2008), initially vague, and ill-defined. The first part of the task of creating a solution or strategy innovation, therefore, is to properly formulate the problem. The method designers often use to clarify the vague and ill-defined problems they get is to question the initial representation of the problem and the basic assumptions that surround it. For example, if an architect was considering the design of a new building at a university s/he would start by questioning the basic assumptions of what happens in a university by asking some disarmingly simple, and often confronting, questions such as: What is teaching? What is learning? What is an office? What is a faculty? (Boland and Collopy, 2004). Wake (2000) suggested that regardless of the type of problem under consideration, designers must ask questions at the start of the design process such as,

> What is the essence of the problem? What is the essence of the prior solution (if any)? Where did the prior solution fail? If it did not fail, how can the prior solution be improved upon? What other ways might there be to do this? Are there other problems similar to this one? What form does this solution imply? What other forms or basic approaches might work as well?" (p. 1).

Defining the brief at the start of the design process is often an opportunity to go back to, and explore those basic assumptions that have become invisible and unnoticed, yet are at the core of the real reasons we are working on the project in the first place. These fundamental assumptions are often unarticulated and keep us from seeing innovative solutions and options. "A designer looks for the real thing we are trying to accomplish, unvarnished by the residue of years of organizational habit" (Boland and Collopy, 2004, p. 9).

> It does not pay to underestimate the power of conventional thinking. It forces you down a ravine. So the question, 'Should we try this other path?' is nonsense because there is no other path. Everybody around us sees that as clearly as you. (Andrew, Designer and Management Consultant)

When people have been doing things a certain way for a long time they rarely are willing or able to go back and question them at a fundamental level. That is why, for example, the first cars were horse-less carriages and the bicycle seat (or bicycle saddle as it was still referred to when I was a child) is still most usually shaped like a small horse saddle instead of being shaped like something that the human backside would actually be comfortable sitting on for more than fifteen seconds. We find it difficult or even impossible to explore our basic understanding and views of something, and the assumptions upon which they are built. We are all busy people, and we are often unwilling to challenge our overall approach. Instinctively that is what good designers do, however.

> The main thing is to know where the client is coming from. Develop it [the brief] with them as they often do not know themselves. Be sure to contradict the brief later. Make explicit the assumptions and challenge them later. (Frank, Graphic Designer)

> I identify the assumptions and then deliberately break them. (Ron, Graphic Designer)

Designers are not afraid to go back to the beginning and the basics, and to question everything as part of the briefing and design process. In order to develop strategy innovations or to solve any ill-defined, complex problem, we must ask fundamental, naive questions as well. This is necessary to solve the problem, and it is why the answer is not obvious and is difficult to find in the first place. Consider the following story that illustrates the value of going back to the basics and questioning everything:

> I was doing an IT strategy project for a large industrial distributor with total sales over $1 billion, with two divisions, each with over 300 branches and I sat down with the general manager and said "What are your hopes with respect to IT?" He said "I have to drag my branch network into the 20th century; I have to get these guys managing their businesses systematically. My number one goal is to help them by giving them a system that provides them with the business intelligence to give to their branch managers." He said "This is what I mean. All I want is a report every week that shows my branch managers on Monday morning at the touch of a button who their top 20 customers were based on trailing four-week sales. Now today my IT system can't do that." So I went to the IT director and said, "So, the GM wants this all-singing all-dancing

business intelligence system." The IT director said "Okay." I ask how much that would cost. The IT director said "Lucky for us we already have a state-of-the-art data warehouse that collects transaction level data 24 hours-a-day and uploads from branch into head office. The problem is that it is going to cost $20 million and take nine months to put in place the network and the new systems so that that intelligence can get back out to the branches." So I asked myself "How is it possible that a corporation this size can have a state-of-the-art data warehouse that already has two years of qualified and cleaned transaction level data but this is going to take nine months and cost $20 million?" I asked the IT manager that question. He said, "The problem is that the GM wants this at the touch of a button. Our network is one way... asynchronous. The only way to do that, I need a high-speed synchronous data network. Today it is called broadband. If we are going to do this we need to replace all the computers we use at the branches because they can't handle the asynchronous communications." So I asked "What if the GM was okay with your printing out the information on a Sunday night and faxing a report out to everybody on Monday morning? It's not at the touch of a button but could you do that?" The IT manager said, "Oh sure, we could do that next week." So all it took was somebody spending a few hours to write-up the report format and one month later they had what they wanted. The CEO could not believe that it would be that simple and wondered "How long did the IT manager know that this was possible?" And a month after that the sales of their top 20 customers by branch went up 3%. So make sure you ask the right questions and if you think you've got it then double-check. (Andrew, Designer, Management Consultant)

This questioning of the problem is not the designer being difficult or obstructionist. It results from recognizing the fact that the initial expression of a design problem or a strategy problem is often misleading. By definition, the person with the problem is not thinking about it in a way that allows them to solve it easily or they would have done so already. It is the task of the designer or strategy developer to think about the problem in a new way that can result in an innovative solution. Designing creative solutions is not really anything impossibly amazing. It is a disciplined way of questioning what is going on. It is a way of looking to see if what is perceived as the problem initially really is the problem, before trying to find a solution to it.

Another benefit of this assumption-challenging process is that without this questioning and reformulation of the problem, we may find ourselves solving the wrong problem. Design problems are sometimes misleadingly expressed as a solution (Bernstein, 1988; Edel, 1967; Holt, 1990; Lawson, 2004). Instead of the brief being expressed in terms of objectives or needs, too often the starting point of the design process is a preconceived solution.

> More often than not, the reality is when a client comes to you they already know what they want or they have an idea. (Julia, Architect)

> When I first began training as an industrial designer I had the opportunity of meeting Victor Papanek and he coined this phrase, "Don't ask a designer how to build a bridge, ask them how to cross the river." As a designer you regularly get a brief like this: "I want you to build me a bridge. I want it to be made of bolts and steel. I want it to be painted yellow. I want it to be this long and this wide with this number of elements to it. Can you go away and design it?" That is not design. That is just documenting somebody's ideas. A designer, if they are capable, should ask, "Why do you want to cross the river? Do you want to take things with you? Does it matter if they get wet? How often are you going to cross the river? How many things are you going to carry and how heavy are they?" If you start to ask all the right questions you start to build the parameters by which the right solution should start to emerge. In the end, it might not be a bridge, you may be better off with a boat or a slingshot or a hang glider. The ways to cross the river are almost endless. Most clients don't think like that. They think they need a bridge, it should be strong and they come up with the solution and ask you to design it. (Brad, Museum Design Manager)

> We were doing this house and they said they wanted something to divide up the space between the kitchen and the other living area 'cause there was one large space. So that's what they said they wanted—something to divide it up. Then you ask a few more questions, "Why do you want to divide it up? Is it noise, is it sound, is it washing?" So when they tell you something like that, you keep delving a bit more and asking more questions, then you find out what they really want and you maybe can do it a different way. (Connie, Architect)

While the importance of defining the problem by asking the right questions is often discussed, and examples are given as presented earlier, little is ever said regarding how to actually do it (Holt, 1990). According to Edel (1967) when trying to define the problem we must identify the functions to be performed that underlie the problem. Taylor's (1969) *functional visualization* process helps us get to the core of the issue and to find the functions to be performed that underlie the problem. The *functional visualization* process is simple and is designed to help the thinker focus on *ways* and *functions* (using verbs) rather than on *things* (using nouns) as people often do. This helps us think more creatively because we are not tied down by our preconceived notions of the *thing*. We, therefore, do not have to limit the solution or design to being a line extension or incremental improvement to the existing *thing*. For example, if our problem was to redesign a toaster, a shoe, a restaurant, or a university classroom, in all cases we would likely start by thinking about, and visualizing, the way *things* are today. This would lead us to try to design incremental improvements to existing toasters, shoes, restaurants, and universities with which we are familiar. Instead, if we focused on the underlying *ways* and *functions*, as suggested by Taylor, and focused on designing *ways to cook* a slice of bread, to *cover* the foot, and to *feed* or *educate* people, we would be freer to think more creatively about solutions. This is what Brad the museum design manager was talking about when he said, "Don't ask how to build a bridge, ask how to cross the river." The bridge is the *noun/thing*. The *function/verb* is the underlying core issue—"How can I *cross* the river?"

Redesigning a toaster means starting with an existing toaster and making it bigger, smaller, faster, or whatever. This is what we typically do in strategy formulation (i.e., last year plus 10 percent). When we think about ways to cook a slice of bread, it leaves us open to consider a vast array of options from the low-tech toasting fork used over an open fire while camping, to ways of using existing appliances, to developing entirely new cooking technologies. Similarly, thinking about redesigning a restaurant, a shoe, or a university is seriously limiting to our thinking when compared to the more open questions of thinking about all the ways in which it is possible to feed and educate people or to cover the foot. In these cases the possibilities are almost endless. This is what we need to do in order to generate strategy innovation.

Applied to strategy, when we get vague and ill-defined problems to solve, we must "question the brief" and the basic assumptions that surround it. We must focus on *ways* and *functions* (using verbs) rather than on *things* (nouns). This will help us separate from the past and to be more creative and able to innovate. We must ask "Why? What is that supposed to achieve? What is the underlying function? Why is that important? So what? Why do you care about that?" until we get to the root of the problem, and can identify the core issues, problems, ways, and functions. We will then be freer to think creatively and to create strategy innovations, new business models, and solutions to seemingly intractable problems.

In design there is an obsession with going back and getting the brief right. Design is a tool that has meaning when there is a problem to solve. And you had better get your head around what the problem is otherwise you have no guide posts to tell you if you are getting close to solving the problem. You have to ask the question, "Am I asking the right questions?" You have to ensure you are bringing a variety of different lenses to the conundrum so you are seeing it from different angles. So in conventional strategy it is as mundane as saying "We need to find another $1 billion in revenue within the next eight years." So as a designer you start asking some questions like, "Do you have any preferences for what country you make this money in?" "No," they say, "as long as it's not too politically risky." "Do you have any strong feelings as to what businesses you want us to look for this money in?" "No not really." So after $350,000 in consulting fees you get them to admit that, in fact, they were interested in businesses that they either were in today or were one step away from in terms of the value chain. When I tell that story to designers they are in complete disbelief that that would be a brief. Most people are really bad at articulating what they want and they are almost as bad at articulating what their source of frustration is or what their problem is. Many strategy briefs are just "Find us some extra costs to rip out or find us some extra money to make." It really can be that basic. (Andrew, Designer, Management Consultant)

As clearly as you can, define why you want to cross the river. That is a fundamental thing that design brings as a discipline to our thinking that strategic planning needs to bring to its thinking. Too often strategic plans are actually almost created in absentia of the creation of the plan. "This is what we want the strategic plan to do, now go away and design it." That is like saying "Here is the bridge, now go away and design it for me." Expand your thinking in terms of what you can achieve through the strategic plan. What are the criteria that you can use to assess if it has achieved your goal? Think differently about the idea, challenge them to think and deliberately look for different ways of addressing those issues. (Brad, Museum Design Manager)

The first step in the process of creating strategy innovation, therefore, is to start to work on defining the problem and questioning the basic assumptions that surround it. Focus on functions and verbs rather than on nouns and things. Do not take the presenting problem or existing strategy as given. Question the problem, and identify and question the inevitable assumptions buried within it. For example, let us assume we were presented with a problem regarding public transportation strategy and operations. After talking to several people, we would identify that the initial presenting problem is that buses are too infrequent in certain areas and this is causing serious citizen complaints. Rather than taking this as the problem and starting to work on obvious solutions such as making bus routes more efficient or adding more buses at peak times, we should ask some basic and naïve questions and identify the under-lying assumptions. It could turn out that buses are never actually full so the problem is not that there are not enough buses and the solution is not to provide more, the problem could turn out to be that people do not like waiting for buses for an undefined period of time with nothing to do. The real problems are related to uncertainty of when a bus will arrive and people being bored and feeling like they are wast-ing their time while they are waiting. Our search for solutions now would focus on ways we can provide more accurate information about schedules or provide real-time alerts when buses are within a certain distance from an area, or on changing bus shelters to make them more comfortable, or providing entertainment and distraction so people do not mind waiting. The way to solve the problem, therefore, starts by questioning the brief and exploring the underlying assumptions. We can then accurately define the problem and start the process of finding solutions to it.

Binding: The Discipline of the Brief

For designers, the discipline of the brief is not a rigid discipline but a guiding one. Good design is an iterative process and given the ill-defined, complex nature of design and strategy problems, sometimes the best way to try and define a problem is to start trying potential solutions to see what does and does not work. The new information gained from our research and trials must be considered, synthesized, and resynthesized with our understanding of, and definition of, the problem. This could, of course, be an infinite process. Designers typically are focused on keeping the search for options open as long as possible (Blyth and Worthington, 2001; Lawson, 2004). The problem with typical management decision-making, on the other hand, is that its focus on quickly and efficiently coming to a decision can lead to premature closure, to a narrowing of the number of possibilities considered, and to a lack of creativity and innovation. This highlights the two sides that must be held in dynamic tension by the discipline of the brief. We have the creative impulse of openness and endless iteration, feedback and refinement on the one hand, which needs to be balanced with the practical impulse of decisiveness and closure on the other. The discipline of the brief helps provide this balance.

Allow people from the very beginning the freedom of creating a variety of different solutions without the imposition of "Don't do that for this reason." It is too easy to put people down for why something won't work. Our judicial system, our political system, it is all about argument. That is why we have a government and an opposition; we have a defence and prosecution. The nature of what we do is about creating argument. Sadly, when it comes to design and creativity those arguments get applied too early. It is too easy to pull down an idea. It is much harder to build up the idea. So in strategic planning, CEOs come in and pull down all the ideas to their idea and you have to go with theirs. Whereas, if you are truly thinking strategically that would not be the most creative way to do it. We have to apply the constraints, but only after we've developed a conceptual framework of how it might work. You can go too far the other way as well and you can never come up with a final solution. A famous architect once said "I have never built a building yet that I wouldn't change." Even in exhibition development many times we've created something and look back at the end of the day and say we would do it differently next time. What you do is take that knowledge and carry it forward to your future projects. (Brad, Museum Design Manager)

Why put any constraints or discipline on the project in the first place? Won't the discipline imposed by the brief (e.g., time constraints, problem boundaries) stifle the creativity we are trying to bring to bare on the problem? If we want truly creative strategy innovations why are we not suggesting that people working on the problem be given complete freedom?

> You have all of those constraints on the site and all that information. You have to take that in and try and come up with something that works with them. So I guess that's the most important part of it, getting it all together and coming up with some scheme that works with all of them while still being something that's innovative and works well. (Connie, Architect)

> There is always time pressure on a designer, everyone wants it now. You have to be professional, it is a job, not an art, but the job is to be artistic. (Simon, 3-D Animator, Master Jeweller)

While it may seem paradoxical at first, it is the fact that we have constraints that calls forth our creativity. For example, consider the well-known creativity exercise where you are asked to build a paper airplane that can fly the furthest distance using only one piece of paper. When we do this exercise as part of our executive programs we get many designs of traditional paper airplanes and, since it is done in the context of creativity, almost invariably some people simply "scrunch-up" the piece of paper into a ball. When it comes time for the trial flights, more often than not, the paper-ball actually flies (i.e., travels) the furthest. On one course recently when preparing for the second round of the exercise, someone asked me, "Can I use two or three pieces of paper to make the ball heavier so it will fly even further?" I said, "No, the rule is one piece of paper each." She said I was stifling her creativity. After we discussed it and she and her team tried to work within the constraints, she realized and reported to the rest of the group, that the constraint of *one piece of paper* actually required them to think of creative ways to make it heavier. They tried wetting the paper ball, putting a coin inside it, and so on. It was the constraint on the problem, not complete creative freedom that required them to come up with the creative solution.

> Sometimes budgets should be seen not as a constraint but as an opportunity to magnify your ability to create things. (Eberto, Architect)

> The best thing you can do to a creative process is put some discipline on it. (Philip, Industrial Designer)

While not always appropriate in every situation, other constraints that should be considered during the briefing stage are performance criteria defining what we mean by success and how it will be measured, business and financial objectives, project timescales, launch date, activity timescales, project scope (i.e., what is inside and outside the areas of concern), and any relevant regulations and standards (e.g., ISO, government regulations). According to Thackara (1997), "Stringent performance criteria are in the best interests of both designers and clients in the longer term. Defining—and sticking to—precise targets for time, costs, and quality should be the automatic basis for relationships between designers and clients" (p. 435). This critically important factor for carrying out a successful design project, therefore, lies with the client not with the designer because only the client has the essential contextual information (e.g., industry and business sector knowledge and experience) necessary to establish relevant performance criteria (Boyle, 2004).

Designers are telling us, therefore, that for successful strategy creation we need the discipline of boundaries and parameters on the one hand (e.g., definition and measurement of success, business and financial objectives, project timescales, boundaries, activities, standards), balanced with open minds and creativity on the other, to help us creatively generate options for strategy innovation.

An Idea Worthy of Pursuit

While trying to establish an accurate and shared understanding of the problem, purpose, or goal of the project as part of the brief, we must also assure that we have an idea that is worthy of pursuit that will motivate those tasked with its achievement. When designers look to establish the purpose of the project within the brief they often develop a hierarchy of nested purposes:

Develop a purpose hierarchy (array(s) of purpose statements from small to large wherein each larger one describes the purpose of its predecessor) from which is selected the purpose(s) the solution should achieve . . . Setting up purposes in a hierarchy in the first phase pushes a . . . project immediately into exploring alternative reasons for the effort, expanding the solution space, and selecting the biggest purpose/function which the project can seek to achieve with the "best" possible solution. Pursuing this right at the beginning . . . is essential because there is no way of knowing when starting whether or not a "breakthrough" solution can be attained . . . This also provides much greater assurance that a purpose which needs to be achieved will be selected, the project will have a worthwhile "pay off," avoids working on the wrong problem, and establishes proper priorities for various projects and functional components. (Nadler, 1980, p. 304)

Cross (2000) also suggested ordering a listing of objectives or needs into sets of higher-level and lower-level objectives in terms of importance. He implicitly suggested that in this hierarchical arrangement you might be answering the questions "How?" or "Why?" when going in either direction (i.e., going toward a lower-level of abstraction, toward a more micro, smaller, "within the organization" perspective, or toward something related to an individual; or going toward a higher-level of abstraction toward a more macro, larger, "beyond the individual or the organization" perspective to the level of community or the society at large). For example, if we want to develop a radical new strategy for our telecommunications business, we must ask the following types of questions and explore the related hierarchy of nested purposes worthy of pursuit:

Why? (going macro)
Answer: Because we want to increase market share, increase profits and increase shareholder returns.

Why? (going macro again)
Answer: Because we want to help people communicate.

Why? (going macro again)
Answer: So people can have richer, more meaningful lives.

OK, that seems to be an end-point worthy of pursuit that provides boundaries (i.e., using telecommunications to help people live richer, more meaningful lives) and is open enough to allow many non-traditional, creative options for generating strategy.

Now let's change direction. If we want to develop a radical new strategy for our telecommunications business focused on how we can help people live richer, more meaningful lives, we ask the question:

How? (going micro this time)
Answers: This would lead us to think about ways to stay in constant touch with loved ones, ways to connect with relevant communities of interest, ways to get information, advice, and/or coaching or counselling. Another line of thought might lead us

to consider how mobile devices can be designed to help people stay safe when they walk home or back to their cars alone at night providing light, and acting as a personal defence device or alarm. We might develop a service solution designed to provide personal identification or GPS tracking for any number of applications.

This bidirectional (micro and macro) questioning of objectives establishes a rich hierarchy of needs and goals that leads us toward a purpose worthy of pursuit and toward some innovative areas for strategy creation we may have never considered before.

> So what I tend to do is establish a vision for every project that I do. I think that's really important so everybody knows what we're aiming for. And a vision is just a broader statement of what we want to achieve. And the bigger you make that statement the better it is, and they see it. It's not achieving what you want or what I want, it's finding the balance that will create a very good product and achieve a win/win situation for the people involved and for the people that are coming after. A lot of people forget about that. We tend to think about what's happening today and we tend to forget about who is going to be using this in a year's time? You're usually aiming for three, four years but what happens in fifteen years, who is going to be the user of that? Is the lifestyle that we have right now, one that they will like in the future? Or, is the lifestyle that we have right now, that we've been living for so many years, is it a sustainable way to do it? ... So really I think we need to sit down and think about if it's a good quality of life and we also need to think about how that is affecting the future generations coming. (Eberto, Architect)

Consider what Hamel (1997) had to say about bringing in passion, and an idea worthy of pursuit, to the strategy development process:

> We've too often ignored the emotional side of strategy. If strategy is partly about collective purpose and a sense of shared destiny, don't we need to recognize this explicitly in the way we go about creating strategy? For example, has anyone out there looked explicitly at the issue of commitment? I don't mean the

commitment of financial resources by senior executives, but the emotional commitment of individuals at the bottom of the organization who are being asked to devote their lives to carrying out a new strategy. (p. 77)

If we want the efforts, energy, and commitment of those we are asking to devote their lives to carrying out a new strategy, we must give them a goal worthy of pursuit. Once again, designers give us an excellent example.

[A]nd that involves the architect not only doing the building, but going into the details and that gives you a sense of ownership of your project. I remember one of my clients came to me and invited me to his opening for his house. While I was there I turned to him and said, "Well, you might have paid for this, but really it is my house." (Eberto, Architect)

This is the type of passionate ownership, identification, and commitment we want from the people developing and executing strategy in our organizations.

Principles: How People Conduct Themselves in Pursuit of the Purpose

Once we have identified a worthwhile, binding purpose, we must consider the underlying principles of behavior we want to bring to bear on the problem. According to Archer (1979) in the inaugural issue of *Design Studies*, "there exists a designerly way of thinking and communicating that is both different from scientific and scholarly ways of thinking and communicating, and as powerful as scientific and scholarly methods of enquiry, when applied to its own kinds of problems" (p. 17). The principle underlying this "designerly way" of thinking and communicating is the distinction between people who have a *design attitude* and those who have a *decision attitude*.

Design Attitude versus Decision Attitude

People who have a decision attitude are problem-focused and they try to find the one hypothetically optimum solution (Cross, 1982). They approach problem-solving by identifying and then choosing among alternatives using tools such as cost benefit analysis, risk assessment, and multiple criteria decision-making (Boland and Collopy, 2004). Scientists and decision-makers in business typically problem-solve by analysis. This analytical, problem-focused decision attitude works well in clearly defined and stable situations when alternatives are identifiable. A decision attitude works well with "tame" problems (Conklin, 2006; Rittel and Webber, 1973) such as "What is the shortest distance between A and B?" or "Which is the most popular color for a toaster?" but not for complex, "wicked" problems or for many strategy problems. A decision attitude works well in stable environments when the future is a linear projection of the past and present.

When trying to develop strategy innovations, however, by definition the future is not a continuation of the past. When dealing with wicked strategy problems, it is not possible to gather and analyze enough data or the right data. The solutions are not known or are not knowable, and there are often no objective criteria against which to judge the best solution (Conklin, 2006; Rittel and Webber, 1973). In these cases, it is not possible to use a decision attitude, problem-solving approach successfully because it is not possible to identify and then rationally choose among alternatives. It is not possible to problem-solve by analysis and to find the one hypothetically optimum solution because the solution must be created not found.

When trying to solve wickedly complex problems, therefore, designers do not follow the logical, rational (or bounded-rational) "waterfall" pattern (Conklin, 2006; Cross, 1982; Lawson, 2004) of gathering and analyzing data, then formulating solutions, choosing, and then implementing the best solution. Instead, designers "start by trying to understand the problem, but they would immediately jump into formulating potential solutions. Then they would jump back up to refining their understanding of the problem. Rather than being orderly and linear, the line plotting the course of their thinking looks more like a seismograph for a major earthquake" (Conklin, 2006, p. 9). In other words, designers work simultaneously or iteratively on understanding the problem and on formulating a solution. Nonlinear design thinking often is as iterative, creative, and complex as the problems being dealt with.

Designers are not necessarily decision- or problem-focused. They adopt a design attitude rather than a decision attitude. Designers use a problem-finding strategy based on generating and testing potential solutions rather than a solution-focused, problem-solving strategy trying to find the one best or right answer as we typically do in strategy and business more generally (Cross, 1982; Lawson, 2004; Liedtka, 2000;

Wake, 2000). Designers bring disparate things together to generate novel solutions. They are more concerned with proposing a series of options, and with having those eliminated, until they find one that is acceptable (cf. Brown, 2005, 2008; Kelley, 2005). They want to create a large number of diverse solutions, rather than focus on finding the one right answer. According to Martin (2005c), great designers seek deep understanding of the user and the context, which entails consideration of many variables. Great designers do not limit their considerations to aspects that can be thoroughly quantified. They worry less about whether they can replicate a particular process (i.e., reliability) and more about producing a valid solution to the problem before them. Designers are, therefore, focused on exploring what works and what might be possible, rather than on analysis of what already exists. This is especially important when trying to generate novel strategy innovations as this approach is more likely to yield multiple and creative options.

Another difference between an analytical decision attitude and a design attitude is that designers learn and know by doing (Lawson, 2004). They are activity and action oriented and quite often visually oriented. For example, many designers tend to think actively with their pencils (Liedtka, 2000).

I use large sheets of paper and colored pens and I doddle. I think from my shoulder. (Alison, Physical Work Environment Designer)

I always start by sketching, which is the great shorthand. It helps me to visualize things. (Jorge, Design Educator)

I work, I draw and I change modes. (Karen, Architect)

This does not mean that strategy developers all need to learn to draw. It does suggest, however, that a great deal can be learned through action and experimentation. In strategy development, our decision attitude tends to focus us on finding the one best solution and on reaching a decision as quickly as possible. This tends to keep us from "doodling," sketching, playing, and exploring many options and, therefore, from being as creative and innovative as possible.

Boland and Collopy (2004, p. 5) related the quintessential example of the difference between a design attitude and a decision attitude in their story about business school professors (i.e., with a decision attitude) working with an architect (i.e., with a design attitude) on the design of their new business school building. They had to reduce the floor space by about forty-five hundred square feet. Quite rationally and predictably, they first identified a number of communal utility spaces that had to be squeezed into the smaller design such as closets, restrooms, storage areas, and spaces for copiers and printers.

> There were many constraints to be met including proximity to classrooms and offices, "ownership" by various departments and research centres, and circulation patterns in each area. We went through the floor plans, beginning with the lower level and working our way up to the fifth floor. The process took two days.
>
> Working with large sheets of onionskin paper laid on top of floor plans, we would sketch possible arrangements until we had something we all agreed was a good solution. Then we would transfer the arrangement in red pencil onto the plans. Each move of one element affected others and often required backtracking and revising previously located elements. Many times during the two days, we would reach a roadblock where things were just not working out, so we would start with a clean sheet of onionskin and try a different approach. At the end of two days, it was a tremendous sense of accomplishment to have succeeded in locating all the required elements into the reduced floor sizes. We were working at a large table and Mat [the project architect] was leaning far into it, marking the final changes. As he pushed back from the table, we were joking about how tedious the process had been and how glad we were to have it over. As we joked, Matt gathered all the sheets of onionskin and the marked-up floor plans, stacked them, and then grabbed an edge and tore them in half. Then he crumpled the pieces and threw them in the trashcan in the corner of the room. This was a shock! What was he doing? In a matter-of-fact tone, he said, "We proved we could do it, now we can think about how we *want* to do it."

This design attitude is also illustrated in the following quotes from two of the architects interviewed:

> It is easy to get a detailed brief and simply fulfil it. I like to think that maybe we could do something better. (Catroina, Architect)
>
> Instead of just taking it [the brief], you go back and have a look at how you can make it work better, so you look at the whole scheme again and look at what else you could do... Instead of just doing

the easy thing, we go back to the basics. We know we can do that so that's not interesting, what's interesting is designing something. (Connie, Architect)

Like Matt the architect in the example given earlier, Catroina and Connie are not focused on, nor satisfied with, just making a decision and quickly solving the problem (i.e., they do not display a decision attitude). They want to experiment, explore other options, and find out how they can do things better. Their design attitude is a key to their creativity, lateral thinking, problem-solving ability, and success. Similarly, if we want to create radical, innovative strategies, products, and services, experiences and industries that break the rules and run counter to convention, and that are so useful, interesting, and noteworthy that they cannot help but be successful, strategy innovators must adopt a design attitude as well.

Another way of looking at this difference between a design and a decision attitude is to consider that traditional business people and strategy developers are concerned with proving that something "is" or "must be," while designers focus on exploring what "may be." According to Liedtka (2000), "Design thinking deals primarily with what *does not yet exist*; while scientists deal with explaining what *is*. A common theme is that scientists *discover* the laws that govern today's reality, while designers *invent* a different future" (p. 14). Designers create and invent choices rather than discover existing truth. This style of thinking is critical to the creative process. In other words, designers are primarily concerned with the future and "what might be," "what may be," and "what could be." These are questions that are at the heart of the creative process. They are essential for the development of strategy innovation required by a world in which the future must be actively created and is not a linear extension of the past that can be analyzed and/or uncovered.

Therefore, key elements of a design attitude are a questioning of basic assumptions and a resolve to leave the world a better place. Designers relish the lack of predetermined outcomes and they tend to approach each new project with a desire to experiment with materials, technologies, and methods, and to do something differently and better than ever before (Boland and Collopy, 2004). This is exactly what creating strategy innovation by design means. We must relish the lack of predetermined outcomes. We must work creatively within the established boundaries. We must approach each new project with a desire to experiment and do something differently and better than ever before. We must be willing to continually experiment with possibilities, ideas, materials, technologies, methods and more. We must not be satisfied with what we did last year plus 10 percent or something that will make us some money and leave our planet, our communities, and/or our employees worse off. Finally, we must question our most basic assumptions and always resolve to leave our people, our organizations, and our world a better place than we found it, thus ensuring we are following our design attitude principles in pursuit of a worthy goal, and better engaging the hearts and minds of those tasked with making the strategy innovation happen.

People: Who Needs to Participate

The third element of the brief is people. There seem to be two views regarding who should be involved in the definition of the problem and the formulation of the brief, and who needs to be involved in the early stages of the design process. The first view is that, in practice, the designer is often handed a brief or a problem. In this case the question of involvement in the establishment of the brief is moot.

The second, more ideal view is that numerous stakeholders (i.e., members of the design team as well as diverse representatives from relevant stakeholder groups such as production/service delivery, technical areas, finance, marketing, etc.) need to be involved in developing the brief (cf. Bernstein, 1988; Blyth and Worthington, 2001; Boyle, 2004; Bruce and Bessant, 2002; Design Council, 2006). This diversity of inputs is considered important to ensure a broad range of ideas and concepts are proposed and because design team members will understand the brief better if they have been involved in developing it.

I found that they were more receptive to our ideas if we made them part of the design process and then made them feel as if they were their ideas...The funny thing was I think by them going through the whole process of designing it, I think they realized just how difficult it is. You know when you present them with a piece of paper, with a drawing, it's like "oh yeah, that works" or "that doesn't work" and I think they started to understand just how hard it was. (Julia, Architect)

It is a problem when the design team is brought in far too late in the experience. When we first moved into our building, the group with the contract to do the work started two-and-a-half years ahead of when the in-house exhibition design team were brought in, so what we ended up with was a difficult situation where we had to almost try to retrofit the building while it was being built. It would have been better if we had been together as a team from the beginning. I know of several regional museums that are faced with the same problem now. City Councils start building the building, often with a limited brief from the institution about what they are going to use the building for. The result is they wind up having to retrofit the building that is under construction...a complicated situation. (Brad, Museum Design Manager)

Similarly with strategy development, a diversity of inputs is important to ensure that a broad range of ideas and concepts are considered and because those involved will understand the brief and the process better if they have been involved in it. Diverse teams are consistently shown to be better at management decision-making and problem-solving (cf. Prichard and Stanton, 1999; Yu, 2006) as diverse teams do more planning, have a greater number of interactions, and have lower consensus (i.e., higher levels of creative abrasion).

"The key to success therefore lies in ensuring that the brief and all project parameters are clearly articulated, communicated and observed by all contributors from day one. The brief is the central nervous system of successful design" (Boyle, 2004, p. 13). This point about needing to communicate project parameters and the brief to key stakeholders is especially critical when talking about the design of strategy innovations. The best way to communicate project parameters and the brief to key stakeholders is to involve them in its development in the first place. While it is not always possible or preferable to involve everyone affected by a strategy or a decision in its development, instead of tending to err on the side of involving as few people as possible in strategy development as we seem to do now, we must err on the side of involving as many people as possible if we want to create and implement innovative strategy successfully.

According to Blyth and Worthington (2001), however, "One of the problems with managing teams during briefing is that they are composed of individuals representing different organizations. They have different agendas and priorities" (p. 84). While this is a benefit in terms of generating ideas and trying to think creatively, it can sometimes make decision-making during the briefing process challenging.

For example a conservator wants to take the object, put it in a black box in acid-free paper and lock it away in cold storage because that is the safest way to protect the object. The designer, on the other hand, wants to take it out-of-the-box, put it on a pedestal, hit it with a thousand lux of bright light and make it rotate. Often the brief is all about compromises in some degree. The trick is understanding where you are compromising too much, versus where you are ignoring significant aspects. (Brad, Museum Design Manager)

Regardless of the acknowledged difficulties, successful strategy innovation requires creativity and, therefore, a diverse range of inputs. Everyone who has potentially important knowledge and experience, including customers, suppliers, shareholders, and a broad cross-section of internal stakeholders from the bottom to the top of an organizational hierarchy, and from sales and marketing to production and service delivery to accounting and finance, not just the senior team, must be involved. In order for innovative strategy creation to be successful, many new voices bringing new perspectives must be heard in a dialogue that cuts across traditional organizational boundaries releasing a deep sense of discovery and passion within many people resulting in a willingness to try new things (Hamel, 1998).

Concept: A Set of Relationships among People that Allow for the Pursuit of Purpose in Accordance with the Principles

The fourth element of the brief has to do with relationships between critical stakeholders. There are two important sets of relationships that allow for the pursuit of purpose; the first is the relationship between the organization/client and the designer, and the second is the relationship between the organization/client and its customers.

Organization and Designer Relations
According to the Design Council U.K. (2006),

The relationship between the designer and the organization or department that has commissioned the design work is crucial. The best relationships are a two-way street, where each party is receptive to the concerns of the other. The designers should be sensitive to the practical concerns the client expresses and, if they are from an outside agency, understand that the client knows more about the detailed issues of the particular industry and market than they do. On the other hand the client should give the designers' ideas a fair hearing and grasp the opportunity to think differently rather than rejecting on sight anything that might at first seem too radical.

This give-and-take is critical, because if we are to design innovative, breakthrough strategies, by definition the suggested strategies will be well outside of what is considered the norm for the organization and the industry. This means that without awareness of this issue, there is a good chance the suggestions will be rejected for being too radical. In many organizations, when trying to introduce radical, creative ideas, we get reactions such as the following:

• It is too new.
• We do not do that kind of thing.
• It is not proven.
• It could go wrong.
• We had better stick with what we know...

If there is a single area of the company where creativity is essential it is where ever the direction of the company itself is set...Because of [the] strongly internalized approach, strategic decision-makers may find it hard to take the step...This is a mistake, however, as creativity can and should have a major impact on the development of strategy. (Clegg, 1999, pp. 65–67)

In order to be truly innovative you sometimes have to do things "180 degrees different from standard management practice" (Sutton, 2004, p. 269). For example, instead of hiring fast learners, people you like and with whom you feel comfortable, and people you have a specific need for, Sutton (2004) suggested hiring people who are slow learners of the organizational code, people you dislike, and who make you feel uncomfortable, and people you do not think you really need. Of course, this only makes sense if you want creativity and innovation. If you want people to do things differently, you must hire people who do not conform, people who are different, and, therefore, bring diversity to the group, as well as people who have some "slack" time to innovate. This, however, is often difficult to do (cf. Bozionelos, 2005; Lim, Winter, and Chan, 2006), especially in times of economic downturn.

Organization and User/Customer Relations

A key to successful strategy innovation is keeping pace with, or getting ahead of, your customers. Jung and Cherng (2005) suggested that we look

> beyond traditional products, market categories and segments, and develop an "anthropological" view of key customers and their needs. Think of consumers as individuals. Watch their moves. Know their buying history. Understand what they value and what they will pay for that value. And, most important, engage your customers (and channels) in your customer experience improvement efforts.

In other words, give up your organizational perspective when developing strategy and take on the customers' perspective.

Strategists cannot develop strategy innovations solely by looking at themselves, their organizations, their industries, and their competitors. They must give up their focus on their perspective and on what is now, and take on the customers' perspective and dream about what could be as well. One way to move from an organization-centered to a user-centered or customer-centered view is to be concerned with the question, "How can we develop a strategy (or business model or service experience) that is less reflective of our existing internal business structures, processes and existing products/services, and more reflective of the customers' existing and future needs and goals?"

> You go into the field and you ask the customers why they buy what they buy, particularly why they choose one firm over another. And you do a life-cycle analysis of the purchase and the life-cycle analysis gets you out of the corporate boundaries and into the client's or the customer's space...In a sense, you have to do an econometric analysis of your customer's business so you know how you can help them do their business. That is the basic. Go look at your customers' customers and find out what they are really buying from us or what they hope they are buying from us. (Andrew, Designer, Management Consultant)

Andrew is right. In order to create successful strategy innovation we must look outside our organizational boundaries and beyond what already is there, and take a customer, community, and/or societal, global perspective.

Unfortunately, few strategy developers do this. As we discussed earlier, if our problem was to redesign a toaster, we would likely start with an existing toaster (noun/thing) in mind and look for ways to make it better, when we should be starting by thinking about the almost endless ways to cook a slice of bread (verb/function). Similarly, when we are creating strategy innovation, instead of thinking about how things are now in our organization and our industry, and looking for ways to improve them, we must focus on our customers, communities, and social structures and on the almost endless ways we may be able to serve them better.

Structure: The Charter that Creates a Legal Entity

Structure and control are the fifth important element of the brief. According to Hock (1999),

> By structure I mean the embodiment of purpose, principles, people, and concept in a written document capable of creating legal reality in an appropriate jurisdiction, usually in the form of a charter and constitution or a certificate of incorporation and bylaws... details of eligibility, ownership, voting, bodies, and methods of governance. It is the contract of rights and obligations between all participants in the community.

In other words, structure in this sense is about legitimation, power, responsibility, and authority. The question for us at this point is "Who should have control, power and authority over which aspects within the design process and what should be left uncontrolled?"

Where Structure and Control are Needed

So far, we have identified a number of areas where structure and control are definitely needed within the strategy innovation by design process, for example:

- Design or strategy development projects cannot succeed without a clear vision of what they are trying to achieve. This direction must be championed at a senior level and someone must be given specific responsibility for it at that level (Carlopio, 1998, 2003; Oakley, 1990).
- Clear boundaries must be set regarding the definition and measurement of success, business and financial objectives, project

timescales, boundaries, activities, standards, and so on (Boyle, 2004; Thackara, 1997).

• The development team must be diverse and representative of a number of key constituencies such as managers from across functions, employees from a number of functions, as well as customers, suppliers, government regulators, and other relevant stakeholders (Bernstein, 1988; Blyth and Worthington, 2001; Boyle, 2004; Bruce and Bessant, 2002; Design Council, 2006).

This will not happen naturally. It will take discipline and a conviction born of the knowledge that strategy innovation will not succeed as well without clear vision, goals, boundaries, and a diversity of inputs as it will with them.

Where Structure and Control is an Inhibitor
There are also many areas where structure and controls are most definitely not needed and would be counterproductive to the strategy innovation process. According to Clegg (1999),

Few companies are yet to go the whole hog and accept the creative organization. It is a concept which is still emerging. Although in principle any company could change the way it works so radically...Many organizations will continue to be held back as long as the top team is holding on to an old-fashioned concept of central control. Without giving up a considerable part of this traditional power it is impossible to achieve the flexible, small-unit approach. (p. 52)

For example, senior managers must relinquish their stranglehold on the strategy development process. Strategy cannot be kept a secret if it is to be formulated creatively and successfully implemented once developed.

A related issue to consider during the briefing stage has to do with sources of power, authority, and status. Consider the following from Martin (2005a):

The primary source of status in traditional firms is the management of big budgets and large staffs. When executives have the occasion to boast about themselves, they tend to refer to the number of people for whom they have direct responsibility and/or the bottom line that they deliver each year—for example, "I run a

5,000 person organization, and our bottom line this year will be $700 million." And of course, bigger is always better! In a design consultancy, the source of status and pride derives from solving "wicked problems"—problems with no definitive formulation or solution and that have definitions open to multiple interpretations. This reality is confirmed by the appearance of the office of any star designer: Desks, credenzas, and shelves are covered with the "best" designs—the ones that solve the most difficult design challenges in the most elegant fashion. Designers become known for their great solutions, whether the Apple mouse, the Bilbao Guggenheim, or the Nike swoosh. These designers enjoy the highest status inside their firms and across their industries. As a consequence, everyone in the design field seeks to earn status through tackling and solving wicked problems, not administering the biggest budgets or the highest number of people.

Designers seem to be concerned with achieving results, not with controlling inputs. This idea that designers actually like difficult challenges, and derive their power and status from solving them successfully, is illustrated by van Gaalen (2005). In his article on extreme engineering he described how engineers and designers tackled the problem of designing the British Antarctic Survey's new research station. The station had to be a great place to live and work to attract the best scientists in the world. It had to provide good living and working conditions, and it had to be safe. It had to protect inhabitants from brutal weather conditions as the Antarctic is a barren place where it is pitch dark for 105 days of the year. Instead of shying away from such a difficult project, engineers and designers from around the world seemed to be drawn to it as there were eighty-six expressions of interest. The chosen lead designer was purported to be enjoying every minute of the project and said, "This is by far the most exciting thing I have ever done." In many organizations, status, power, and authority are often formally and hierarchically derived. This must change in organizations trying to create strategy innovation.

Practices: Deliberations, Acts, and Decisions within

the Community that Animate and Update the Design

The final elements of the brief are the practices that drive behavior. From designers we learn that the most essential practice that animates their efforts is allowing them the freedom to be active and creative. According to Hock (1999, p. 12) this final element related to our practices is a reminder that we must avoid binding participants (i.e., designers or strategy innovators) to any one practice (i.e., one prescribed design or strategy development method), no matter how desirable it may appear. We must encourage experimentation, and allow designers and strategy innovators to decide how best to achieve the purpose within the broad boundaries we set.

There are many ways to create significant value for customers, organizations, our society, and our planet. As we know, there is no single solution, product, service, or strategy that will work for everyone, and there is no one right way to develop them. Ways to achieve strategic competitive advantage, as Porter (1980) articulated so successfully, are to focus on differentiation via uniqueness, to be focused on being low-cost or to be a niche player. Still another way to achieve strategic success is to focus on innovating to deliver category benefits better and more reliably than anyone else (Barwise and Meehan, 2004).

There is a time and place for radical strategy innovation that "wins" and "wows" the customer, and makes a significant positive difference in our world, but that is not the only way to innovate strategically. There are other ways to innovate by being radically better, for example, but not necessarily radically different. Doing something "better but not different" means that your product or service does what it is supposed to do more reliably or better than anyone else's. The innovation in this case is in the design of a system that delivers unparalleled reliability of service or of product performance, rather than in coming up with something no one has ever thought of before. It is more focused on being better than on being unique (Barwise and Meehan, 2004). The key is still to connect with the customer, but instead of focusing on creating something new, there are times when we must focus on finding out how well we are performing relative to our promises and customer expectations, and how we can do what we do significantly better. For example, when Orange entered the telecommunications market in the United Kingdom, they focused on delivering "a reliable, high-quality customer experience with good value for money" (p. 25). With this "simply better" strategy they have been more successful than either of the incumbents or the other new entrant.

What both the uniqueness and reliability perspectives have in common (i.e., the essential practice that animates and updates the design) is their focus on strategy innovation. They are not concerned with strategies that are the same as last year plus 10 percent or with incremental improvements to existing production/service delivery or with product/service line extensions. We already know how to do that (e.g., TQM, six sigma). All of our efforts (i.e., our deliberations, acts, and decisions) must be focused on allowing people to innovate and to figure out how to make radical leaps and step-changes, whether they are in pursuit of competitive advantage via strategy innovation, by being drastically better and more reliable, or via uniqueness, niche, or low-cost positions.

CHAPTER THREE

Research: The Art of Seeing the Different Way

Few, if any, in the management and strategy development area (in practice or academia) would consider it reasonable to try to create strategy in the absence of adequate information regarding such things as markets and competitors. Similarly, according to studies by Badke-Schaub and Frankenberger (1997), "in the design process [the] non-availability of information was a crucial factor responsible for deficient analysis of solutions" (p. 361). There seems to be general agreement, therefore, that it is important to research widely to ensure that you have adequate information available before proceeding to develop your options and choose a solution or strategy. Typically, however, the research that is done as part of a traditional strategy formulation process and that which is done as part of the design process varies in both their purposes and their methods.

In this chapter, therefore, we will first look at the purposes of research in the traditional strategy development process. We will then examine the purposes of research in the design process and explore how design research can help us gather information that is critical to successful strategy innovation. Finally, we will discuss design research methods that can help us explore problems in new ways, help us connect with our customers, and provide insights for the development of more radical strategy innovations.

Traditional Strategy Development Research

Of course, many authors and practitioners concerned with strategy development discuss the importance of research. Within the traditional strategy formulation process research is undertaken to understand the market, the competition, ourselves, and our organizations. For example, within the popular "positioning" view of strategy development, research often involves assessment of elements in the organization's external environment such as competitor behavior, market structure and potential, and market share. The majority of research is focused on "analysis of each significant existing and potential competitor" and on "forecasting future industry conditions" (Porter, 1980, p. 71). Numerical data are typically collected and analyses conducted to determine the "right" answer (i.e., the best market position as defined by the position being unique, inimitable, valuable, rare, defensible, etc.). Research is used in this case for the confirmation of hypotheses or for the justification of decisions.

However, this "environmental analysis—no matter how rigorous—is only half the story. A complete understanding of sources of competitive advantage requires the analysis of a firm's internal strengths and weaknesses as well" (Barney, 1999, p. 128). Therefore, proponents of the more internally focused resourced-based view of strategy have stressed the importance of looking at an organization's existing resources, competencies, and capabilities before developing strategy (Barney, 1991, 1999, 2001; Chakraborty, 1997; Zehir, Acar, and Tanriverdi, 2006). Porter (1980) also suggested looking internally, "Once the forces affecting competition in an industry and their underlying causes have been diagnosed, the firm is in a position to identify its strengths and weaknesses relative to the industry" (p. 29). However, researching our own organizations in addition to our competitors is still not researching the whole story. The customer is sorely missing.

While customers are most certainly important to strategists, rarely is it suggested that customers (existing or potential) be researched beyond trying to gain understanding of such "technical" aspects as their relative power within an industry or their demographics, segmentation, and current or projected spending capacity. One noticeable exception is Prahalad (1993): "How can firms create totally new products and services? [by] Understanding the 'meaning of customer-led.'—In most firms, this means listening to customers and giving them what they ask. That's important, but it is also important to lead customers…leading customers is what competing for the future is about" (p. 47).

Leading customers means knowing what customers want, even before they do, providing it for them and then leading them to it. Unfortunately, as customers ourselves, most of us are not able to accurately predict the social structures and institutions, industries, technologies, products, or services upon which we, and the majority of others, will be dependent in the future. Our future needs and behaviors are difficult to predict because they are hidden or latent. No statistical analysis or experiment, no matter how valid and reliable the data it yields, can help us make these predictions either.

Design Research

Ferreting out latent customer needs, however, is one of the areas in which design research excels. This is the first of the two ways in which traditional strategy research and design research differ significantly. Designers know how to do research that yields in-depth knowledge about peoples' behavior, needs, emotions, preferences, and reactions. "It turns out that people do not always behave as they think they behave: they tell you about how they operate, but when studied closely, they operate in significantly different ways, though they are not aware of it" (Vedin, 2005, p. 296).

From a design perspective, "research is the art of seeing the different way" (source unknown). This is the second significant difference between the purposes of research in strategy and design. Unlike research done in the traditional strategy development process and the social and physical sciences, where research is often solely used to try and identify the right or best answer, research within the design process is also used to gather information so designers can see different perspectives, as well as generate and explore different options. Each of these two areas of difference will be discussed in more detail in the two sections that follow.

Research to Explore and Better Understand the Problem

A significant difference between traditional strategy research and design research is that designers often conduct research to explore an issue, problem, or potential solution and to gain information, insight, and understanding by doing so. This is something frequently overlooked in traditional strategy research. As discussed in chapter two when we looked at the brief, the presenting problem is often taken as "given" and assumed to be straightforward, linear, and solvable, when the problem should be probed and assumed to be multifaceted and involving many complex interrelationships and unknown aspects that could be explored fruitfully. Research in design is often done to help solve the problem by gathering information and ideas that help designers in the concept generation and prototyping phases of the processes that follow. Research is, of course, also done later in the design process to evaluate the functionality, usability, and success of designs and this will be discussed in chapter six. Designers at the start of the design process often conduct research more to look for information, to clarify their thinking and ideas, and to spur creativity than to look for the one right answer and to confirm or reject hypotheses in an experimental sense.

Ideation is done by research. (David, Graphic Designer, Design Educator)

I start with research—who is my customer, what is the competition like, what are the trends?...gathering all the parameters of the project. I would then summarize this info into a product definition document. (Tony, Industrial Design Manager)

The first step usually involves finding inspirational images that relate to the product I'm about to design. It is a visual form of research that gets you acquainted with the market. It allows you to find trends and decide how you are going to make your product better and more unique. (Kacie, Industrial Designer)

Without proper research, one does not have the proper knowledge to make sound design decisions. (Jim, Industrial Designer, Art Director)

I start with basic research around the theme...internet, literature, exhibition catalogues, magazines, talking. (Elisabeth, Communications Designer)

Just my mind, thinking, discussing with our customers—they give a lot of ideas and if their ideas are close to my ideas, it helps a lot. Seeing what is in the market and not to do it. This is very special way to work because I sell as well, but it is very useful to get feedback all the time. (Anne, Product Designer)

Our minds aren't as clever as nature to create bizarre things, you know, so you're just sort of constantly researching on that and I love that. (Angelo, Architect)

Research is a creativity technique. We have in our minds a stock version of a cat or Moscow, what they look like, it is a cliché without research. What is in our mind is precede, a summarized version of the real thing. I need to see the real and the raw thing. To be creative you need to feed your self first-hand. (Rod, Illustrator and Design Educator)

A good way to summarize this first difference between traditional strategy research and design research is to consider how Lester, Piore, and Malek (1998) distinguished between the analytical and interpretive management approaches. The analytical approach is basically a linear, rational, engineering approach. You start with a problem that must be solved. You define clear objectives based on research into customer needs. You identify the necessary resources (e.g., human, financial, technical) and any constraints on those resources. Finally, you divide the problem into a series of discrete components and assign each to an appropriate expert (Lester, Piore, and Malek, 1998). The interpretive approach, on the other hand, views the process more as an emerging conversation and is more aligned with how research is used as part of the design process. It is concerned less with analysis and problem-solving and more with interpreting the new situation. People are concerned with listening to, and talking with, customers and other stakeholders, as well as experts. They are focused on discussing new possibilities that open up through these conversations. This interpretive process is one of invention and is highly creative. "To encourage and harness that creativity, the manager of the interpretive organization needs to act less like an engineer and more like the leader of a jazz combo. Diverse components need to be brought together... The goal is not to arrive at a fixed and final shape but to channel the work in a way that both influences and fulfils the listener's—the customer's—expectations" (p. 89).

This is reminiscent of the decades-old debate regarding the relative value of research that is exploratory, frequently reliant on qualitative methods, and focused on theory building, versus experimental research that is focused on quantitative methods and on theory testing. "Theory testing occurs where an existing theory or hypothesis is taken as the guide to a piece of research and is then tested using methods that will allow it to be measured and evaluated... In contrast, where the emphasis of research is on theory building then the purpose of a study is to seek out meaning and understanding of the phenomena" (Carson et al., 2001, p. 11). Theory building research is not necessarily aimed at finding solutions and answers. This type of prospecting research is often looked down upon in the social sciences as second-rate "prairie empiricism." As a result, authors who use or discuss exploratory, qualitative research methods are often unnecessarily apologetic or defensive about them; for example, "given the much discussed prominence if not dominance of quantitative research currently, it is helpful to recall that qualitative analysis was the primary means by which virtually all social research was conducted up to about mid-century" (Gummesson, 2000, p. ix).

While exploratory research aimed at theory building and the use of qualitative research methods have their detractors, they most certainly help designers identify challenges and possibilities, come up with creative solutions, and solve the problems on which they are working.

> Often we don't know exactly what we want, so it really is best to just go in and look around to find out...Design as a process is in the business of creating possible solutions rather than reducing sources of possible risk, rather than reducing avenues. In the absence of any clear direction you have 360° of options to choose and you cannot afford to pursue them all. A strategy process tries to equip you with arguments and the evidence to narrow that 360° down, at least down to 45° if not 22.5°. The interesting thing about design is it says "There are 360°, so what? What if I show you something like this at 0°? What if I show you something at 180°? What happens if I show you something at 90°?" That is a different way of cutting the pie. (Andrew, Designer, Management Consultant)

> We explore who the customer is and what the use scenario is so we can identify the strategy and the next opportunity, what the position is relative to competition and what the future potential is...most of this is done with visuals. The most effective method is to bring the consumer/user into the room by providing film clips from in home or in-store ethnography, and then show story-boards, computer renders or models. Models are always preferred for more refined designs; sketches and one act plays for the up-front. (Mark, Industrial Designer)

"I have been asked whether I support the quantitative, allegedly more 'scientific' methods, or whether I reject them in favour of a qualitative approach...I am neither a priori for nor against any methods. They should be used where they are appropriate" (Gummesson, 2000, p. 2). The question for us, therefore, is "Where are qualitative and quantitative research methods most appropriate when trying to create strategy innovations?"

Qualitative research and theory building is useful when trying to interpret information. Quantitative research and theory testing is useful when trying to determine the right answer or test a specific hypothesis. When faced with something new or not well known or understood, therefore, qualitative research methods are more appropriate (Carson et al., 2001). Qualitative research methods allow us to explore relevant issues, identify important factors and boundaries, and determine in which broad direction(s) to proceed.

Consider the following from Vogel, Cagan, and Boatwright (2005, pp. 54–55) that illustrates a situation in which traditional quantitative research methods cannot be used to help us find the right answers. In this case, exploratory research using qualitative methods would be more appropriate:

> In the Adidas 1, the censors assess the sole's compression, affected by weight, terrain, and runner's speed, but the design team could also have included a pedometer and calorie counter... Should the Adidas 1 include a pedometer? In other words, would sales be higher if the model had a pedometer, or lower, or would it even matter? Until this is tested, the answer is unknown. Although the current shoe is not equipped with a link to a desktop or laptop, the in-shoe computer could conceivably have an outlet to download information into a laptop. What would happen to sales? Or the shoe could have a wireless transmitter to send data to a hand-held PDA. Would sales be higher? Similarly, the design team has chosen to show off the circuitry via a clear plastic panel, but that, too, was a factor that could have been optimized. How are costs affected by the clear panel? Will sales be higher? Adidas's first smart shoe did not need to be designed for running—it could have targeted soccer, a sport Adidas has long dominated and a core area of its expertise. The possibilities are seemingly endless. Each decision can be tested in an experiment, like a test market. But not all decisions can be tested; there are just too many. Without market tests that would show which integrated features are the best combination for the marketplace, it is not clear what exact product the company should develop to achieve the greatest improvement to the lives of customers and to the company's bottom line. The answers to the choices (exact product specifications) are ambiguous rather than clear... because information is lacking, but decisions still must be made. Decisions here are not safe, and ramifications of decisions are unpredictable.

In this case, since it was not possible to run controlled experiments employing rigorous data collection and statistical analyses to confirm or disconfirm predetermined hypotheses and find the rationally optimal configuration of features and right answer, it was best to interview a number of lead-users or to have one or more of the design team join a local running club and explore the situation through participant observation. These qualitative research techniques are better able to generate useful information, perspectives, ideas, hypotheses, insights, and outcomes that can be used to inform and guide choices.

Before you draw a line you have to go and live with the client and understand exactly what they want. It doesn't matter if the guy wants to build his holiday house in the country or a big company, you have to go and understand how they function because in that way you will be able to tailor-make solutions for them and make solutions that are functional for them. (Eberto, Architect)

Researching the Customer: Identifying Latent Needs and Emotions

The second significant difference between the purposes of research in design and strategy is that almost unanimously, successful designers are customer-focused (i.e., user-focused in the language of design) and they also almost always attempt to gain a deep understanding of the customer that goes well beyond a knowledge of their demographics, physical and functional needs to determine their deeper emotional and psychological reactions and unmet, latent needs (Drew and West, 2002; Fulton Suri, 2005; Holt, 1990; Martin, 2005b, Norman, 2004). This allows designers to lead customers by identifying latent needs as well as researching what customers currently do and say they want. Because people are often not aware of the deeper emotional and psychological aspects of their behavior, they are not always aware of the many options that are available for their fulfillment. This is what is meant by a latent need (i.e., an unrecognized, unmet, nonobvious, dormant, or underlying need or value).

Traditional strategy developers are quite good at identifying what has been and what is, and then extrapolating what might be. As already discussed, this works well when the future is an extension of the past. Our linear, quantitative research methods are excellent at identifying trends in customer preferences and then helping us to justify appropriate strategic line extensions and incremental adjustments. They are not good at helping us generate something new and inventing an innovative future. They are not good for developing strategy innovation.

In other words, traditional research methods can help us identify basic, essential, and expected needs, features, benefits, or services (such as clean sheets on a hotel bed or an efficient check-in process at a hospital), because these features and services exist and are already expected (Wagner and Hansen, 2004; Wood, 2004). It is much more difficult to identify latent needs because they are, by definition, unexpected, unrecognized, and unmet. Unfortunately, we cannot always ask our current customers what they would like as they sometimes do not know or cannot articulate what they want or need. For example, Henry Ford is supposed to have said, "If I had asked my customers what they wanted, they would have said 'a faster horse.'" Once again we see how people tend to focus on defining the problem in terms of wanting to improve the existing "thing" (i.e., the noun, as discussed in chapter two) because horses were the predominant means of transportation, when the designer focuses on the underlying function, need, or value (i.e., Henry Ford focused on the verb—transportation—and innovated by developing a breakthrough means of powered transportation).

The value of identifying latent needs and underlying functions is that they can provide insight for the creation of strategy innovation just as they have been used for years to provide insight for new product development. For example, according to Dodgson, Gann, and Salter (2005), "collaboration with customers and end-users results in improved product development processes in many industries. When product and service suppliers forged deep relations with particular customers, they are sometimes able to create 'robust' or 'dominant' designs" (p. 131). These dominant designs bestow a significant, lasting competitive advantage upon those who create or capture them. Similarly, Lajocono and Zaccai (2004) stated, "Design is understood as a core activity conferring competitive advantage by bringing to light the emotional meaning products and services have, or could have, for consumers and by extracting the high value of such emotional connections" (p. 75). This is a key aspect of design research that can benefit those of us concerned with strategy innovation. Deep customer understanding provides raw materials for the generation of creative solutions, new business models, and new industries.

Consider the following from Bell (2004b), an anthropologist from Intel, who spent two years doing field work in seven Asian countries to find out how people from different cultures think about and use technology in order to help Intel's new product developers design future technologies:

> I don't go in asking questions about technology, because it's easy to miss things that turn out to be relevant later. For instance, if you went in asking questions about the Internet and computers, you might miss something about say, the importance of filial piety and ancestor worship in traditional Chinese culture—which in turn frames everything from people's ideas about education, to their ideas about wealth and money. You wouldn't necessarily see that, but it turns out to be important in the ways people think about and use new technology. (p. 3)

Kelley (2005) suggested that when we connect at a deeper level with customers and identify their latent needs, we are able to act as "experience architects" designing compelling experiences for customers that go beyond merely fulfilling existing needs. When developing strategy, strategists rarely, if ever, consider their customers in this way. For example, when Porter (1980) discussed customers' needs and behaviors, he did so mainly in terms of their concentration and purchasing power.

> An industry's buyers can also differ in their purchasing needs. Different buyers may require differing levels of customer service, desired product quality or durability, needed information in sales presentations, and so on. These differing purchasing needs are one reason why buyers have different structural bargaining power. (p. 109)

While theorists, practitioners, and researchers have realized that having a customer orientation, staying close to your customers, and using various methods to try and identify their underlying needs is critically important for success in new product development, in reinventing business processes and business models, and in building entirely new markets (Drew and West, 2002; Fulton Suri, 2005; Holt, 1990; Martin, 2005b; McGregor, 2006), it is not at all easy to do (cf. Norman, 2004).

> With increasing demand for product quality, influenced by greater user awareness, consumerism and legislation, the provision of proper information about user needs is an important aspect of the design process. This is now commonly recognized. Millions

of words are written each year about the importance of market orientation, of bringing the user's problems and needs to the center of the planning process. However, it does not appear that the many words have had much impact on industrial practice. (Holt, 1990, p. 201)

A strategist might think it natural to turn to marketing colleagues to identify practical and well-regarded research methods that can help enrich his or her understanding of the customer. Unfortunately, while excellent at assessing existing needs and practices, market structure and potential, and market share, traditional marketing research typically does not provide insights into latent needs and their underlying functions, values, and emotional components (Ante, 2006; Burian, 2005; Fulton Suri, 2005; Gummesson, 2000; Holt, 1990; Martin, 2005a; Walton, 2006). According to Lajocono and Zaccai (2004),

Traditional consumer research—surveys, focus groups and so on—asks people what they want. However, while customers can reliably express their preferences for incremental improvements in existing products and services, they cannot reliably express their higher-order needs and aspirations, which may call for radical redesign or for entirely new offerings. Although these higher-order aspects are what form the basis of a customer's emotional connections to any offering, the customer himself may deem them irrelevant, insignificant or even embarrassing, or may simply not be conscious of them. (p. 76)

In order to assess latent needs, underlying functions, and emotional meanings and connections, we must turn to more qualitative research methods favored by designers.

What can those of us interested in creating strategy innovation learn from the ways designers conduct research? As discussed earlier, we learn first that we must integrate people from a variety of backgrounds into the design research team. This diversity is critical as it ensures multiple perspectives are represented. Second, we learn that our strategy research teams must use a variety of research techniques to help them better understand what people really think, do, and feel, not just what they say they do in their daily lives. This search and researching must involve a mix of traditional quantitative research tools (e.g., telephone polling, surveys, interviews, focus groups, archival document collection and analysis) and qualitative research methods derived from the social sciences (e.g., psychology, sociology, anthropology) such as field research, observation, hidden cameras, and a "reading" of a culture via its magazines, TV programs, Internet sites, and chat rooms (cf. Bruce, 2002). These latter methods focus less on objectivity and more on a sense of participant observation because they rely a good deal on interpretation. These and other qualitative research methods are the focus of the following section.

Design Research Methods for Strategy Innovation

Traditional marketing and strategy-related research methods for gathering data are such things as surveys/questionnaires, focus groups, brainstorming, interviews, and archival document collection (e.g., company reports, industry studies, trade magazines, business press; cf. Porter, 1980, appendices A and B). In terms of methods, design research is often much more qualitative and exploratory than quantitative or experimental. Design research methods tend to focus on observation and exploratory research to stimulate thinking and creativity, and to identify opportunities, ideas, emotions, and latent needs. Design research methods allow us to do several things traditional strategy research methods do not: (1) gain a deep understanding of customers' behavior to identify current and latent needs, and the functions and values that underlie them; (2) identify the emotional meaning and emotional connections customers have with a service, product, company, or industry; and (3) explore and better understand the problem on which we are working, allowing a more holistic view of the problem and facilitating more creative solutions.

Qualitative Research Methods for Strategy Innovation

Qualitative data collection methods provide information to help identify customers' actual and latent needs and desires, as well as provide information allowing us to holistically explore and better understand problems so we can then design and test new ways to meet those needs and desires (Lajocono and Zaccai, 2004). "This is surely the era of customer-centric design—an era in which psychologists, anthropologists, and sociologists are often included on design teams, and ethnography and anthropometrics are trusted research methods" (Seidel and Pinto, 2005, p. 1). Ethnography has received some good "press" recently (cf. Basu, 2008; Clark, Smith, and Yamazaki, 2006; Kane, 2007; Nussbaum, 2006; Seidel and Pinto, 2005; Walton, 2006; Wareham,

Busquets, and Austin, 2009). Ethnography is the subfield of anthropology focused on describing specific human cultures. For our purposes, it is important to realize that we are discussing rigorous scientific disciplines that have been used to research various aspects of human cultures for over one hundred years. These research methods are well tested, valid, and reliable and they tend to be more holistic than numerically focused traditional strategic analysis methods.

I would say that the core of our research revolves around rapid ethnography, whereby we do one-on-one consumer interviews and/or observe them in action. Our interviews and observations are highly structured. They are not just a conversation and hang out. We deploy many tools and always document the process. (Brian, Industrial Designer)

We do a lot of research to verify and identify things. We do rigorous analytical human factors research, and we do ethnographic interviews and observations. (Philip, Industrial Designer)

According to Bell (2004a), an ethnographer at Intel, "Ethnography's hallmark is this notion of participant observation, the idea that you learn about other people's cultural practices by going there, being there, and by doing it with them. Most traditional anthropologist, who would consider themselves to be ethnographers have spent years living in other cultures with people, and not just watching what they do, but actually doing it, too" (p. 3). Many people are familiar with Jane Goodall, who spent decades living among chimpanzees studying their behavior and society, and with Margaret Mead, a pioneering anthropologist who spent years in Polynesia. Mead's writings were accessible to laypeople, and she and Goodall popularized ethnographic observational research methods to gain insights into the behavior and culture of their subjects not just because their subjects could not fill out questionnaires, but because they were trying to gain deeper insights into behavior, cultural beliefs, and values that surveys, industry analyses, and archival documentation could not provide even if they existed. These qualitative research methods allowed them to observe and analyze group values and behavior in its cultural context. They were able to focus on "*what* people in a cultural group do, *how many* of them do it and *how what they do* affects the individuals in the group [because] What defines us as human beings is that, despite the differences across cultures, we are all trying to create meaning in our lives" (Laabs, 2003, pp. 31 and 34). Culture and context provide important cues to meaning and interpretation. Language provides only part of the message. The context in which something is used or done affects its meaning and use (Chamorro-Koc, 2008). It is this "meaning" that we need to discover if we are going to design strategy innovations successfully.

Counting and classifying can take us only so far. Meaning and interpretation are required to attach significance to counts and classifications. By collecting a mixture of field notes of personal observations and commentary, taped interviews and meetings, and company documentation, various qualitative methods can be combined with traditional quantitative methods to fruitfully provide a source of rich and naturalistic data (cf. Eunni, Kasuganti, and Kos, 2006; Gummesson, 2000; Laabs, 2003; Lynch, 1982; Ormerod, Rummer, and Ball, 1999; Tashakkori and Teddlie, 2003). According to Martin (2005c), great designers consider many variables in their quest for deep understanding of the user and the context. They do not limit their considerations only to aspects that can be thoroughly quantified. They seem to use any methods they can think of that enable them to get into the heads of customers, to illuminate the customers' thinking and emotions, and allow them to deeply understand and empathize with customers as ethnographers do (Bell, 2004a; Laabs, 2003).

Consider the following hypothetical example (adapted from Nussbaum, 2004) of the application of design-inspired research techniques to the development of strategy innovations. Here is a typical strategic scenario:

The Board, and everyone, agrees that you must grow. Profits are flat. Market share is, at best, stable. You are, of course, concerned about existing competitors and potential new entrants. You commission some market research and begin a series of internal meetings at senior levels to discuss strategic opportunities for growth. Based upon serious consideration, scores of discussions, the best market research data money can buy, and all the information and intelligence at your disposal you decide to try and enter a new market with your existing services by rebranding and repositioning yourself at a slightly lower cost while counting on significant volume increases to make up the difference. You also put some money towards the development of a promising new idea. (e.g., new product or service)

Let us see how the story changes when we employ a number of design-oriented research techniques trying to gain a deep understanding of our customers' experience:

The Board, and everyone, agrees that you must grow. Profits are flat. Market share is, at best, stable. You are, of course, concerned about existing competitors and potential new entrants. [Here is where our stories diverge.] If you were developing strategy for a hospital, you would start by talking to hospital managers, doctors, nurses, facilities managers, etc., as well as customers and competitors (if possible) about what is currently happening and where current products and services are working and fulfilling expectations and conscious needs, and where they are not. You would use traditional research methods such as interviews and questionnaires to gather quantitative data and conduct analyses as usual. In order to start to identify new opportunities and latent needs, however, hospital managers, doctors, nurses, facilities managers, etc., as well as customers would observe patients and their families as they make their way through the hospital front doors, and stay with them observing the process every step of the way until they leave through those very same front doors once again. If you were developing strategy for a University, the University Executives, Heads of Schools and Deans as well as faculty members would all take a class one term and go through the entire process from application, orientation, registering for classes, finding your way around the campus, attending class, doing assignments, and receiving your grade. If you were developing strategy for a professional services firm (e.g., consulting firm, law firm), you would ask senior partners to engage your own firm and go through the entire process as if they were customers.

Adding qualitative to quantitative research methods gives us a better chance of coming up with some amazing insights into scores of ways to improve our customers' experiences and dozens of opportunities for new products, services, and strategic directions, not just ways to extend our existing products and services or ways to incrementally improve our bottom-line. Consider the following case example of the results of qualitative observational research in a hospital (adapted from Nussbaum, 2004):

We found that patients and family often became annoyed well before seeing a doctor because checking in was a nightmare and waiting rooms were uncomfortable. We found that doctors and medical assistants sat too far apart and that many people, especially the young, the old and immigrants, visit doctors with a parent or friend. Unfortunately, that second person is often not allowed to stay with the patient, leaving the afflicted alienated and anxious. Patients hated examination rooms because people often had to wait alone for up to 20 minutes "naked," with nothing to do, surrounded by threatening equipment and needles. They concluded that the patient experience could be awful even when people leave treated and cured. Hospital management realized its long-range growth plan did not require building lots of expensive new facilities. What it needed was to overhaul the patient experience. They learned that seeking medical care is much like shopping—it was a social experience shared with others. So it needed to offer more comfortable waiting rooms and a lobby with clear instructions on where to go; larger exam rooms, with space for three or more people and curtains for privacy, to make patients comfortable; and special corridors for medical staff to meet and increase their efficiency.

Those described in Nussbaum's (2004) hospital example realized that they were designing human experiences, not buildings, and that in order to achieve growth they did not need to make huge capital expenditures and buy expensive new medical and information technology or increase the number of beds by 50 percent. They needed empathy, a deep understanding of the users' experience, and the resultant radical shift in the way they thought about the business they were in and the products, services, and value they provided to customers.

The people at IDEO[1] seem to be obsessed happily and profitably with gaining empathy for their customers (cf. Fulton Suri, 2005; Kelley, 2005; Nussbaum, 2004; Weiss, 2002). According to Pink (2003),

> In the IDEO universe, great design doesn't begin with a far-out concept or a way-cool design. It begins with a deep and empathic understanding of the human condition. The first step for any IDEO team on any project is to try and empathize with the people who might use whatever product or service that eventually emerges from its work. (p. 104)

From the IDEO method cards[2] we can see that IDEO has identified and uses four broad types of nontraditional qualitative research methods grouped under the headings of learn, look, ask, and try. We will discuss a number of design-oriented nontraditional and qualitative research methods in more detail under each of these four headings in the subsections that follow.

Learn: Collect Information and Analyze it to Identify Patterns and Gain Insights into Customer Behavior and Needs

A central feature of design activity is a preoccupation with geometrical patterns or some other ordering principles or "codes" that must be imposed in order to make a solution possible (Cross, 1982). What designers tend to do well is to see associations, identify and/or make relationships, and form them into patterns. For example, great designers are able to predict the next cultural mood and identify trends (Meagher, 2006). Bruce (2002) discussed how it is important to "braille" a culture (i.e., reach out to touch, feel, and sense) when trying to forecast trends. This cannot be done solely from your office nor can quantitative research provide an answer. It takes a mixture of reading, researching, and thinking as well as a lot of searching, fieldwork, then doing, looking, listening, and searching some more.

> Successful design is all about picking out trends. You will start to notice that a square shape, that is strong and simple and easy to use, shows up in a number of different places—in fashion, in interiors, in products. In fact, trends and patterns repeat themselves in almost predictable historical cycles. That is why we study the history of design and we are always looking in magazines. (Kim, Interior Designer)

The process of pattern recognition is more than just connecting-the-dots to reveal the underlying pattern waiting there to be discovered. It takes effort, knowledge, creativity, and imagination to find and assemble the pieces, to fill in the gaps where bits are missing, and then to interpret it all within the appropriate context. "Designing is a process of pattern synthesis, rather than pattern recognition. The solution is not simply lying there among the data...it has to be actively constructed by the designer's own efforts" (Cross, 1982, p. 224). Once again, we see that designers are skilled at and focused on creating and generating something new rather than discovering what already is. This is what makes their processes and methods so valuable to those of us concerned with strategy innovation.

Pattern recognition: The art of finding order in chaotic masses of data
Whether we realize it or not, humans are naturally well equipped to identify and recognize patterns. For example, we can recognize a song from only a few notes (aural recognition or "name that tune"). We can recognize people from a great distance or after not seeing them for many years (visual recognition). We recognize many scents and we remember them for long periods of time. When we recognize that people have personalities and behavioral traits, we are using a form of cognitive pattern recognition. We perceive patterns in peoples' behavior and preferences that are consistent across time and different situations, and we call it their personality (e.g., introversion, or extroversion). Similarly, when we create and choose a strategy, we are recognizing existing patterns and trends in our external and internal environments based on our analyses of the recent past and present, and then making future plans in relation to them. When we try to create radical strategy innovation, however, the patterns are not obvious; they are latent. They are not there for us to uncover. We must creatively and actively construct them; we must design them.

In order to identify patterns successfully there are several things we must do. Coutu (2002) suggested that a key to successful pattern recognition is to ensure that we always consider the context. Bernstein (1988) has suggested we think of design as applied perception. The designer has to take into account and relate the way things are perceived and the way in which they exist objectively. They relate the thing to its perception, its purpose, and all within the context in which that object is being used. It is not easy to sort through the millions of bits of information with which we are bombarded, take into consideration the context in which they occur, and then arrange the relevant bits into a meaningful coherent whole or pattern.

When bird-watchers look for patterns to enable them to recognize species, for example, they must ask themselves "Where am I?" and "What time of year is it?" (Coutu, 2002). Two similar looking birds can be distinguished, given a certain time of year and place, by whether you find one sitting still atop a tree or constantly flitting from branch to branch. Certain things are more or less likely to happen in certain situations or following other events, and we must take these contextual factors into account when looking for patterns. For example, if your market share as a percentage of sales via your traditional distribution channels has remained steady for a significant period of time, you could read this as a signal that all is well. The pattern seems like business as usual. Unfortunately, if you do not investigate the wider context and explore what is happening in your nontraditional distribution channels, you might miss the fact that sales of competing products via your non-traditional channels was growing faster than your sales via traditional channels (Schoemaker and Gunther, 2006). The pattern now looks quite different.

It is also important to remember that pattern recognition is never 100 percent. We are looking for trends and tendencies. Especially when concerned with strategy innovation and, therefore, latent needs and hidden patterns, the generalizations we are making cannot ever be close to perfect or 100 percent accurate. One way to improve accuracy, however, is "triangulation," that is, getting data from multiple sources (Carson et al., 2001). For example, if you get data from your observations, from the popular media, and from two different interviewers all pointing toward the same pattern, you would be more confident in the identification of the pattern than if you based your predictions solely on your observations. This topic will be addressed again later in this chapter when we look at the topic of interpreting qualitative data.

Another key to pattern recognition success is to remember that pattern recognition is a two-stage process. First, we must identify as many potential patterns as possible. This is critical for strategy innovation success and it requires thinking creatively, broadly, and holistically. "If there is one thing we can truly say about managerial decision-making from 50-years of research it is that the weak link is not in deciding among the options on the table, but in getting the best alternatives on the table in the first place" (Yetton, 2006). Once we have as many potential patterns as possible on the table for consideration, in the second stage we can then initiate a process (e.g., nominal group technique, multi-voting) to help us choose which we think are the most likely, important, and impactful patterns.

Pattern recognition and strategy innovation
Pattern recognition is an essential skill for successful strategy innovation. Hamel and Prahalad (1995) suggested that to be successful at strategy development we must spend significant portions of our time (i.e., 20–50 percent) trying to gain a deep understanding of technological, demographic, regulatory, or lifestyle trends and discontinuities that could be used to transform industries, and create new competitive opportunities and strategy innovations. Unfortunately, even though many of us realize how important pattern recognition is for business success, it is still difficult especially at the more macro strategic and industry levels where data are more amorphous (Coutu, 2002).

For example, today's telecommunications companies (Telcos) must look for patterns when they see that:

- The mobile telecommunications market is mature and nearing saturation. The growth of mobile phone use has plateaued. The use of fix-lines/land-lines is decreasing. There are constant price pressures and pressures for product/service bundling.
- There are many uses for mobile communications handsets.
- There are many mobile devices competing in the communications and entertainment markets.
- Netbooks, mobile Internet devices, and mobile phones are converging.
- Technology continues to become more powerful, less expensive, and smaller.
- Early attempts at VoIP (voice over internet protocol) have been successful and are growing (e.g., Skype).

What strategists in the Telcos have to be able to see is an emerging pattern leading to the inevitable decline in the number and use of land-lines/fixed-lines followed by an erosion of the pre-paid mobile market as it migrates to VoIP, and a continual erosion of their profits in traditional areas across their product ranges and markets. That is the more obvious "bad news" pattern. The potential obvious "good news" pattern is the possibility of strategy innovation if they can capitalize on the ubiquity and multifunctionality of handsets and on their increasing functionality, power, and lowered cost.

Telco strategists also have the more difficult task of trying to figure out what else people can and will do besides make telephone calls and send text messages that can fulfil existing and/or latent needs, thus creating new industries and new products/services that will allow the Telcos to generate significant new revenue to replace declining sales. Simply adding a camera, Internet access, and MP3 functionality will not suffice. That is the obvious exiting pattern that is there to be discovered by everyone that will lead to short-term, incremental line extensions. What they need to do is to uncover the underlying functions and latent (i.e., unrecognized, unmet, nonobvious, dormant, or underlying) needs or values associated with telephones and mobile devices more broadly, and base their strategy innovations on the underlying functions and emotional connections they can illuminate, and the value and innovations they can create.

The winners will be the companies that focus on strategy innovation that fulfils latent customer needs rather than on cost-cutting, adding more bells and whistles to existing technology and services, or trying to decide whether 2G or 3G or some other-G is going to dominate technically. Technology will inevitably commoditize network infrastructure, and network ownership will only generate utility returns. Telcos might become personal and corporate "lifestyle brokers." The world may become "device agnostic" as handsets inevitably become commoditized as well. At first, Telcos will be able to charge for some content but eventually this too will become a commodity and most content will be virtually free. People will pay only for convenience, novelty, entertainment, pleasure, meaning, or special required services. New opportunities and profits will be in content aggregation, distribution, management, and billing, and may require Telcos to form partnerships with financial services groups, with technology firms such as Microsoft or Oracle, and with one or two media giants. While this scenario (i.e., pattern) may or may not turn out to be correct, it is an example of several nonobvious generic patterns that are likely to play out over the next few years and how this type of thinking can lead to ideas for strategy innovation.

People such as Slywotzky and colleagues (cf. Slywotzky and Morrison, 2000; Slywotzky and Wise, 2003) have been researching and discussing various "profit patterns" for years. Unfortunately, most of the patterns they outlined are incremental strategic changes, not radical strategy innovations. For example, many of their value chain patterns involve a move to a related adjacent product or sector (e.g., a manufacturer that gets involved in the distribution of their product or a pest-control company that expands into hygiene services). Those of us concerned with more radical strategy innovation can, however, learn a great deal from looking at generic types of patterns. Regardless of your industry, there are several recognizable patterns for which you can look.

Industry-level patterns. There are several patterns of activities that take place in many industries over long periods of time such a convergence, conglomeration, consolidation, and collaboration/cooperation. For example, banking, insurance, and financial services have converged into a financial services industry. Pharmaceutical development has converged with biology and IT/super-computing to create the biotechnology industry. When traditional IT rivals such as Microsoft, Palm, JBoss, Red Hat, and Sun begin to collaborate to try and achieve true integration and interoperability (DiDio, 2005), these types of industry-level changes are groundbreaking and create opportunities for many organizations to undertake new strategic initiatives.

Technical patterns. While many technological patterns are incremental, such as the seemingly relentless march of Moore's Law (i.e., the doubling of the number of transistors manufacturers can fit on an integrated circuit every eighteen months and/or the doubling of computing power per unit cost every eighteen months), these can sometimes facilitate more radical strategy innovations. They can also combine with other patterns to create novel effects (e.g., the case where a cell phone handset becomes so small and inexpensive that it becomes a commodity). Other generic technical patterns that may provide opportunities for strategy innovation are digitization and miniaturization.

Replacement patterns. Of special interest to those of us concerned with strategy innovation, new business models, and new industries are replacement patterns. If we look for alternatives or substitutes to existing products, services, and industries, or for ways to prevent or reduce the need for some products, services, and industries in the first place, we can frequently identify some more radical creative strategic opportunities. For example, if we were trying to reinvent the health care industry and/or solve some of the many problems involved in our current system of hospital care (e.g., the high cost of care or the limited number of hospital beds or the shortage of doctors in certain areas), if we consider substitutes or replacements we can identify opportunities for self-care and/or changing the roles of alternative and allied health care professionals such as nurses, pharmacists, homeopaths, physiotherapists, chiropractors, and so on. If we consider prevention, that leads us down the path of looking at such things as changing our diet, weight-loss, exercise habits, reducing exposure to toxins (smoking, chemicals, etc.) as ways to address certain problems. If we are trying to redesign the transportation industry, for example, by considering replacements, we start to think of ways to replace cars with various forms of public transportation or substitute motor transport more generally with other forms of transportation. If we consider prevention/reduction (e.g., reduce the need for people to travel to work or to meetings in the first place), it opens us up to thinking about strategic opportunities for companies involved in telecommuting or teleconferencing and about the design of our homes, workplaces, and cities in the first place.

Life-cycle patterns. Large-scale life-cycle patterns also create strategic opportunities. The inevitable patterns of birth, growth, maturity, decline, and death create opportunities as organizations and industries move through the cycle. Other life-cycle patterns to consider are commoditization and the productization[3] of services (cf. Slywotzky and Morrison, 2000). Patterns of strategic competitive advantage have themselves, been shown to go through life-cycles. For example, Cagliano, Acur, and Boer (2005) examined three longitudinal samples from the International Manufacturing Strategy Survey database and found that while strategic configurations were relatively stable, many companies changed strategy over time and they were able to identify which patterns of change prevailed. They found that product-based strategy was the most widely spread and stable, while capability-based competition was the rising star. The market-based strategy configuration was struggling and price-based competition was on the decline.

Research methods for pattern recognition and strategy innovation
There are three qualitative or nontraditional research methods we will discuss here that can be used to help identify and recognize latent patterns and help provide ideas for strategy innovation: (1) affinity diagrams, (2) activity analysis, and (3) character profiles.

Affinity diagrams
An affinity diagram is similar to a mind map (Buzan, 2000, 2004) but instead of starting with a central theme and drawing related branches off of it, we start with a number of issues or concepts and we cluster them according to various relationships (e.g., similarity/differences, common elements, meaning, or functions) and we look for the resulting groupings or patterns. It is a well-known method of sorting a number of observations, concepts, or ideas into natural groupings and has been used regularly for many years within the quality movement to help cluster root causes or to structure, analyze, and map the relationships between ideas and attributes (cf. Cohen, 1988; Zimmerman et al., 2006). A "Google" search of "affinity diagram" revealed hundreds of thousands of websites, many providing instructions and examples like these modified from the Vanderbilt University School of Engineering's Engineering Management Program (mot.vuse.vanderbilt.edu/mt322/Affinity.htm):

How to conduct an affinity sort:
1. Conduct a brainstorming session on the topic under investigation.
2. Clarify the list of ideas. Record them on small cards or "sticky" notes.
3. Randomly lay out the cards on a table, flipchart, wall, etc.
4. Without speaking, sort the cards into "similar" groups based on your gut reaction. If you don't like the placement of a particular card, move it. Continue until consensus is reached.

5. Create header cards consisting of a concise 3–5 word description (i.e., the label or unifying concept for the grouping). Place the header card at the top of each group.
6. Discuss the groupings and try to understand how the groups relate to each other.

This process allows us to discover various patterns of grouping and relationships among what at first may seem like a haphazard mass of unrelated ideas. For example, let's start with this list of ten words: suffer, dark, house, quickly, sand, doctor, cold, sweet, cheese, and now. What we are trying to do is to look for various relationships and patterns among the words and to use them as ways to group or cluster the words. "Suffer," "doctor," and "cold" all might be related to health. "Sweet" and "cheese" are food-related words. These are relatively obvious patterns related to the meanings of the words. Less obvious patterns would be grouping "quickly" with "cheese," "suffer" with "doctor," "house" with "sweet," and "sand" with "cold" and "dark." In this case the words are grouped based on the number of letters in them. Another grouping based on a different set of relationships would be "cheese" with "cold," "dark" with "doctor," and "sweet" with "suffer" and "sand." In this case, the words starting with the same first letter are grouped together. This simple example illustrates two points. First, it illustrates the basic premise of looking for patterns and grouping as part of an affinity sort. Observations, impressions, quotes, or any qualitative data can be sorted in this way. A second important point is also illustrated regarding the need to identify obvious as well as nonobvious patterns. Recall the final key to pattern recognition success mentioned earlier. Pattern recognition is a two-stage process. First, we must be open and creative to identify as many patterns as possible, and second, we must then choose from among them. The first stage is essential for success, difficult to do, and requires discipline, effort, and creativity.

Let us look at another example (adapted from an example provided in Cohen, 1988) that also illustrates how affinity diagrams can be used to help identify latent needs and areas for potential strategy innovation. Let us say that our customers have told us (e.g., via interviews, surveys, and/or from our observations) what is most important to them when thinking about purchasing our products (e.g., computers or production machinery). What is important to them are issues such as the following: the number of staff needed to maintain them, the cost of the warranty, any upgrade costs, the initial staff training required, initial purchase price, power consumption when running, cooling/storage requirements, and the cost of repairs. We can see various patterns/ relationships among the concepts (e.g., some items have to do with ongoing maintenance; others have to do with staff). After trying a number of groupings, we might end up with something like we see in figure 3.1.

Prior to this analysis, we may have thought that customers were concerned mainly with the initial purchase price because correlational evidence suggested that if we offered discounts, our sales went up. From this affinity analysis, however, we can start to see some of the latent, nonobvious factors involved. We may conclude that most of what really concerns our customers regarding their initial purchase decision has to do with ongoing costs (i.e., maintenance and people costs) and not the initial purchase price per se. This may lead us to start to think about innovative ways to structure our product and service offerings. We may consider leasing and maintenance arrangements and focus our business there. Alternatively, we may redesign our entire system and software to

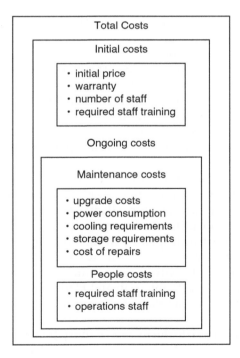

Figure 3.1 An example of an affinity diagram.

reduce ongoing costs for customers and gain a significant competitive advantage that way.

Activity analysis/task analysis
Similar to process mapping, when conducting an activity analysis we try to identify all of the tasks, actions, objects, performers/people, sensory inputs, decision-points, information flows, errors, bottlenecks, and interactions involved in a process. Activity/task analysis is a venerable technique that has been around for many years and is often used as part of process improvement efforts or by those concerned with activity-based costing (cf. Berk, 2006; Ellingson, 1933). A "Google" search of "activity analysis" revealed over two hundred million websites, many providing instructions, worksheets, and examples. While the procedure for activity/task analysis is not standardized, according to Rubinstein and Hersh (1984) every activity/task analysis should address the following questions:

- Who is the user?
- What tasks does the user now perform?
- How is the task learned?
- Where is the task performed?
- What is the relationship between the users and data?
- What other tools does the user have?
- How do users communicate with each other?
- How often do users perform the tasks?
- What are the time constraints?
- What happens when things go wrong? (pp. 25–28)

Our interest in conducting an activity/task analysis is to help us identify opportunities for strategy innovation. For example, the IDEO team analyzed the activities and procedures involved in tooth-brushing, which helped them identify some previously unrecognized needs and concerns.[4] This, in turn, helped them identify opportunities for new products. Activity analysis has been used for decades to identify such things as opportunities for safety improvements and for analysis of system usability and design (Rubinstein and Hersh, 1984; Schultz, 2004). Another example of an activity analysis can be found in appendix, example four.

What we are trying to do during our activity analysis is to build a "use model." A use model is a key to our ability to identify unrecognized and unfulfilled latent needs that can point us toward opportunities for significant strategy innovations. It is a form of myth, metaphor, or analogy that suggests the activities identified have an underlying pattern, relationship, or meaning. In other words, we are looking for ways in which a number of activities, or the activities of a number of different people, can be grouped together because they are related or similar/different or unique. We are looking for a conceptual organizing framework similar to when we think of organizing data on our computers in files and subfiles as in a traditional paper-based office filing system.

> Even if you proceeded with a design without consciously developing a task analysis and a use model, in fact there is always a use model, based on what you, the designer, believe. In the absence of detailed information, we all work from assumptions about who the user is, what he or she does, and what type of system would meet his or her needs. Following these assumptions, we tend to design for ourselves, not for other people. When our assumptions are accurate, we may produce a reasonable system. When they are inaccurate, we may produce the wrong system even though it is well-designed. (Rubinstein and Hersh, 1984, p. 28)

The same can be said about strategy innovation. We may not be aware that we have a mental model or a set of preconceived notions and assumptions when we are developing strategy, but we do. When our assumptions and mental models are "accurate," we develop good strategy. When our assumptions are not accurate, our organizations will suffer as a result.

The identification of these underlying patterns (i.e., the customer's "use models") is our ultimate goal because we will find within them the unrecognized and unfulfilled needs and opportunities for which we are looking. For example, Bartlett and Toms (2005)

> interviewed, 20 bioinformatics experts about the process they follow to conduct a...functional analysis of a gene, and then used a task analysis approach to model the process. We found that each expert followed a unique process in using bioinformatics resources, but had significant similarities with their peers. We synthesized these unique processes into a standard research protocol, from which we developed a procedural model that describes the process of conducting a functional analysis of a gene. (p. 469)

In this case they were able to find the underlying pattern that enabled them to generate a generic process that could be used as a valuable standard and as a teaching tool. This is similar to the process I used to distil the information I received from interviewing designers, and from the design literature, into the strategy by design model used for this book.

Banks could conduct activity/task analysis to identify what customers really need to do when they go to a branch. Airlines or travel agencies could conduct activity/task analysis to identify what customers do when on a business trip as opposed to a vacation. Hospitals and health care practitioners could conduct activity/task analysis to identify what people do when they enter a hospital or a doctor's office. In real estate, activity/task analysis can help identify which rooms people go into first/last and spend the most/least time in. In all of these cases, the patterns of behavioral activity identified can lead to insights into underlying values and latent needs that could, in turn, lead to significant new strategic opportunities.

Character profiles

Another qualitative research method that can be used to help us identify patterns leading to opportunities for strategy innovation is a character profile. A character profile can be built of individuals, groups, organizations, and/or industries. When this is done on an individual, it is a character profile of the salient features of their personality. When it is done on a group, organization, or industry, it is a representation of their collective personality more frequently referred to as their culture.

Individual character profiles can be constructed informally using prose, a collage of images, or an artifact as a symbolic representation (e.g., a pen, a flower, a diaper, a CD). In this case, we would build up a picture, symbolic representation, or description of the target person related to their basic demographic characteristics (e.g., financial position, status, gender, preferred activities, age, life-cycle, values, norms, preferences), and then write a paragraph describing them or produce a collage of pictures cut from magazines that symbolically represent the person in many other ways (e.g., worldview, values, personality, preferences, assumptions, culture, lifestyle, rituals, priorities). Alternatively, a more formal and structured analysis tool and model might be used. There are many patterns of behavior that have been recognized, studied, and formalized into personality types. Some of the most well-known and relevant for our purposes are:

- Traditional Myers–Briggs personality types. There are four dimensions that can be formed into eight or sixteen "types": introvert-extravert, sensing-intuitive, thinking-feeling, and judging-perceiving. A Google search yielded over six hundred thousand websites providing more information on the Myers-Briggs personality types and there are scores of books available on the topic (for more information, see Myers and Briggs, 1998).

- The big five personality dimensions. Many psychologists believe that there are five fundamental personality dimensions that capture the major patterns of human behavior. A Google search yielded about twenty-four million websites providing information about the big five personality dimensions:

  1. Emotional stability. Emotional stability refers to a pattern of behavior we think of as calm, confident, and secure.
  2. Extraversion. An extraverted pattern of behavior would be described as active, excitement-seeking, assertive, warm, talkative, energetic, and optimistic.
  3. Openness to new experience. Openness to experience is characterized by a pattern of behavior tending to be creative, full of ideas, resourceful, imaginative, introspective, insightful, and concerned with aesthetics, feelings, and values.
  4. Agreeableness. Agreeable individuals tend toward a pattern of behavior characterized by such attributes as cooperativeness, straightforwardness, modesty, tender-mindedness, kindness, and trusting.
  5. Conscientiousness. A conscientious pattern of behavior refers to those who have a strong sense of direction, are competent, ordered, dutiful, achievement-oriented, striving, self-disciplined, and deliberate (Adapted from Hunter, 2006).

- Group, organization, or industry character profiles. Based on observations of real people, groups, or organizations we can develop archetypal character profiles (e.g., using prose, a collage of images, an artifact) representing the behavior, personality, culture, or lifestyles of key individuals, customer segments, groups, organizations, and/or industries.

  There are many patterns of collective behavior that have been recognized, studied, and formalized as well. Some of the most relevant for our purposes are related to the concepts of levels of innovativeness and organizational culture. We will discuss each of these in turn.

- Levels of innovativeness (individual and group). Goldsmith, d'Hauteville, and Flynn (1998), Johnson et al. (2001), and Rogers (1995) have illustrated that innovativeness is a recognizable and important pattern of behavior at both the individual and organizational level of analysis that can be measured reliably. Rogers

(1995) identified categories based on the behavior of people and then discussed these groups' socioeconomic characteristics, associated personality indicators, and communication behavior. Rogers' five categories are:

1. Innovators. Innovators (approximately 2.5 percent of the population) are venturesome. Whether they are organizations or individuals they have the time and money necessary to innovate. They also have the ability to cope with a high degree of uncertainty and are risk takers.
2. Early adopters. Early adopters (approximately 13.5 percent of the population) are the embodiment of successful and discrete use of new ideas (Rogers, 1995). They act as opinion leaders and are close enough to the mainstream to act as role models. They are predisposed to try something new.
3. Early majority. The early majority (approximately 34 percent of the population) are not naturally inclined to try something new simply because it is new. "They follow with deliberate willingness in adopting innovations, but seldom lead" (Rogers, 1995, p. 265).
4. Late majority. The late majority (approximately 34 percent of the population) are skeptical of change. The pressure of peers is often necessary to motivate adoption. Most of the uncertainty about a new idea must be removed before they feel it is safe to adopt (Rogers, 1995).
5. Laggards. The laggards (approximately 16 percent of the population) are resistant to change and change agents. Their point of reference is the past. In other words, "If we have never done it that way before, why should we do it that way now?"

• Organization culture. Another well-known pattern of behavior at the organization and group level of analysis is referred to as organization culture. The model based on the work of Cameron and Quinn (1999) is simple yet powerful. It distinguishes four types of culture based on how organic or mechanistic, and how internally or externally focused the group or organization is. They are:

1. Clan: (organic—inward-focused) focus on internal maintenance, flexibility, concern for people, and sensitivity to customers.
2. Adhocracy: (organic—outward-focused) focus on external positioning with a high degree of flexibility and individuality.

3. Market: (mechanistic—outward-focused) focus on external positioning with the need for stability and control.
4. Hierarchy: (mechanistic—inward-focused) focus on internal maintenance with the need for stability and control.

An example of how we can use character profiles to help identify patterns leading to opportunities for strategy innovation comes from some work I did with a global diversified technology and manufacturing organization, serving customers in aerospace, control technologies for buildings, and more. During the project we used several methods to profile the characters of individuals and groups. For example, when we wanted to identify individuals who would act as local champions for the changes we were implementing, we used a questionnaire based on Roger's (1995) levels of innovativeness to identify innovators and opinion leaders. We also asked employees who they thought the influential opinion leaders were in their areas. Once identified, we gave these influencers some extra training and tools, and they were able to act as local experts and champions for us.

We also did several cultural analyses as part of the same project trying to identify meaningful differences in various organizational units and divisions. We identified, for example, one production-oriented area that had a distinctly hierarchy/clan culture and another more sales and marketing oriented area that was considerably more of an adhocracy culture. Once identified, we were able to modify our communication and engagement plans to take into account the facts that because of their external/market orientation, adhocracies are generally more adaptive than hierarchies. They reach out and search for new information, markets, and technology. They try often to expand into new markets, invest in new technology, and emphasize the importance of long-term viability to enhance versatility. They frequently look for information regarding new markets, technologies, and products/services. In adhocracies, therefore, people are more likely to know what is going on in the marketplace (compared to clan and hierarchy cultures) and will be more likely to appreciate the need for the strategic innovation we were implementing. We knew this should significantly increase the success of our strategy innovation efforts as long as we focused on good, basic project management techniques, and ensured that reward and measurement systems were properly aligned, to help provide the structure and discipline necessary to implement the new strategy (cf. Carlopio, 1998, 2002, and implenter.com).

In the hierarchy/clan culture, on the other hand, because of their inward orientation, people were less likely to know what was going

Strategy by Design

on in the marketplace (compared to adhocracies) and, therefore, were less likely to appreciate the need for the strategic innovation we were trying to implement. We knew, therefore, they would need to be given this information. We spent significantly more time on communication, awareness-raising, education, and training with this group. We explained what was going on in the market, why, and how our innovation would address this need. We also knew this hierarchical culture was mechanistic and needed to be unfrozen to help facilitate the implementation of the strategy innovations. These insights were incredibly valuable, enabling us to customize our plans to best match the character profiles identified.

Look: Observe People and Discover What They Actually do Rather Than What They Say or Think They Do

The second set of design-oriented qualitative research methods are focused on observation. Many authors have discussed how designers use a number of observational research methods to reveal latent needs, values, and priorities that help them gain a clear understanding of problems and provide insights into how to redesign (Coughlan and Prokopoff, 2006; Fulton Suri, 2005; Kelley, 2005; Lester, Piore, and Malek, 1998; Reese, 2004). Many of the designers interviewed also discussed the importance of observational research.

Observation of experience is everything. (Guiseppe, Service Designer)

Research is done via walking and observing, listening and seeing. (David, Graphic Designer and Educator)

Ideation is done using observation, being aware of what is around you. (Jorge, Design Educator)

I check out places where people are using or wearing the things which are to be designed. So, when designing a new travel bag, I take a look at the airport, the city, the mall, fairs, etc. ... I need to get an idea what is important and what is not. I need to see people using the things I want to design. (Tim, Fashion Product Designer)

User centred research is done "in situ" rather than in the laboratory context ... good designers take the time to observe customers in their natural environment and they pay attention to the sorts of things that normal business managers do not. They pay more attention to the experience. (Andrew, Designer, Management Consultant)

According to Fulton Suri (2005), observing peoples' unconscious everyday interactions reveals details about how they relate to the world. She described how she and others at IDEO start most of their projects with observations of behavior in its natural setting.

> Teams do this together, along with clients, as a way of learning firsthand about the context, habits, rituals, priorities, processes, and values of the people we are designing for...the idea is to reveal how unexceptional incidents, looked at from an inquisitive stance, can inspire thoughts about design opportunities and consequences. (p. 165)

It is important to go out into the world and observe people because our existing habits and mindsets stop us from being able to gain the insights necessary when sitting in our offices.

> I am a firm believer in doing things outside of my silo. A wide range of experiences in life leads to creativity. (Richard, Graphic and Digital Multimedia Designer)

> Creativity comes from seeing the world differently, seeing the world a different way. (Todd, Interior Designer, Design Educator)

If you try to generate insights into peoples' behavior while sitting in your office, you will certainly have some degree of success if you are applying creativity techniques, but you will have a great deal more success if you actually get out and look around. More than fifty years ago Osborn (1953) said, "Good prospecting calls for an open mind and for wide exposure; and our prospecting should dig deeper than mere sensing. We should delve into the how and the why" (p. 143)

> We use a protocol called ethno-shopno which bastardizes social science by involving large groups of cross functional team members invading homes and shopping situations in real time three-hour immersion experiences. It would be right to call it ethnography...I also like to say that no one's life was ever changed by a power point. Being "in situ" is the best way to learn, understand and create "a ha" moments. (Mark, Industrial Designer)

The "how" and the "why" are important as they can help us to be more sensitive to people's experiences and latent needs, and they give us a good starting point for strategy innovation. When we see things are being done or used in unintended ways, this indicates something about how our products, services, and existing strategies are fulfilling (or not fulfilling) people's needs (cf. Fulton Suri, 2005). This can translate into opportunities for new products and services, new industries, and new business models. Observing people involved in a process, noting how they behave, what tools and technologies they use/do not use, and how they communicate and interact can lead managers and researchers to crucial insights into latent needs, basic requirements, underlying values, and priorities (Jirotka and Luff, 2006; Lester, Piore, and Malek, 1998).

> Very often, you can build an entire strategy based on the experiences your customers go through in their interactions with your organization. The service brands have a horrible habit of focusing on the one interaction where they think they make money. If you are running an airline, there's an awful temptation to focus all of your attention on what it's like to fly a particular route on a particular aircraft. In fact, you can track backward and forward a whole series of interactions that consumers have with you that are very relevant. If you start to map out that entire journey, you begin to understand how you might innovate to create a much more robust customer experience. (Brown, 2005, p. 53)

Staying with the airline example, observation might reveal that there is a class of customer who comes to the airport without a ticket or reservation, or with a ticket for a significantly later flight, and who is not really price sensitive. They may be willing to pay a premium for the ability to purchase a "standing room," no bookings necessary, just walk on like a bus-type of ticket (usually associated with reduced prices rather that increased prices). This could lead to a whole new business and pricing model where planes leave only when they have filled-up (keeping the price very low for the customer who comes early and is willing to wait, and high for the last-minute walk-ons, while fuller planes and maximal seat utilization reap great rewards for the airline).

There are two basic observational philosophies: objective observation and participant observation. In objective observation, we are trying to capture the facts as we see them. We are concerned with who does what, where, when, and how often. This is nothing new to traditional strategy researchers. In participant observation, however, we are immersing ourselves in a culture or set of activities and we are trying to understand why the things that are happening are actually happening. In other words, we are trying to understand what is going on from the subject's (i.e., customer's or user's) perspective. In this case we go "native" and try to gain understanding and insights via our ability to empathize with the person(s) being studied. This is not the way we typically think about conducting strategy research. There are a number of recognized and well-regarded observational techniques that can be used to help strategists empathize with their customers and gain a deep understanding of their experiences such as mapping, a day in a life, and behavioral archaeology that will be discussed in the subsections that follow.

Mapping. There are two types of mapping that are useful in identifying what people do, and the relationships they have with other people, groups, places, and things. The first is behavioral mapping—tracking people's movements over a period of time to identify which areas are used most often or during what periods of time. The second type of mapping is social network analysis/mapping, which has gained popularity within the knowledge management community, mapping the networks of interactions (e.g., who talks to whom, how often, when, for what purposes) within a group by tracking the positions, communications, interactions, and movements of people over time. While peoples' formal hierarchical relationships can be approximated via an organizational chart, their informal roles as opinion-leaders, influencers, integrators, and linkers are not represented there. There is software available (a Google search of "social network mapping software" revealed about fifty-eight million sites related to various social network analysis tools) that can help you to analyze such things as emails, online documents, interactions, and the communication links implied within them.

An example of how considering group interaction networks and how and when spaces are used led to a creative solution for a school and a community group was provided by Nick, an architect I interviewed. He described a project wherein an architectural firm was contracted by a school that wanted several performance spaces and an auditorium designed and built. Unfortunately, the school could not afford the $7.5 million needed for the five buildings they wanted. To help solve the problem, the architects designed an elegantly flexible system that allowed them to build one building with moveable partitions, doors, and seating that satisfied all the school's requirements. Then they realized the school mainly needed the space between 8:30 a.m. and 3:30 p.m. during the weekdays, sometimes in the evenings, and only rarely on the weekends. They collaborated with a neighboring church group that agreed to pay for part of the construction for the rights to use the new space on weekends during its peak demand times. The school was then able to get the facilities it needed through a combination of excellent architectural design and a consideration of group interaction networks, and how and when physical spaces are used.

An example of how peoples' movement can be tracked and mapped can be seen in figure 3.2. It represents the movements of several people in part of an office of a professional services firm over a few hours time. As we can see, the fax is hardly ever used. The library is mainly frequented by TD, who appropriately is situated right outside of it. It is also appropriate, for example, that MC and FF are next to each other as they interact a great deal, and that PR is near RF and the copier. Depending on what the goals of the analysis are, a simple diagram like this can provide information regarding the use of space, and about work, communication, and social networks.

Capture a day in the life. Another technique that can help strategists empathize with their customers is to observe and catalogue (e.g., via photos, video, notes, sketches) the behavior, activities, routines, habits, rituals and physical environments, and so on that users/customers

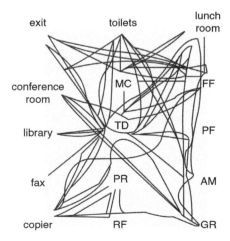

Figure 3.2   A map of staff movements in an office environment.

experience in a day. This can help identify and facilitate an understanding of customers' unexpressed and unmet needs, as well as uncover ways to connect with them emotionally. IBM has used "a day in a life" observational studies to identify what people really carry in their pockets on a typical day, rather than what they say they carry in their pockets, purses, briefcases, and backpacks. The insights gained served them for years after the conclusion of the study. This enabled them to consider such questions as, "Can technology improve or replace some of the traditional items we carry? Can we converge, eliminate, or make redundant such individual pocket items as identification cards, credit cards, multiple keys, PDAs, and cell phones? Are there cultural barriers to implementing particular design directions?" (Clark, Smith, and Yamazaki, 2006, p. 51).

Behavioral archaeology. A third observational technique is to look for evidence of people's values, needs, intentions, motivation, purpose, attitudes, beliefs, culture, and activities inherent in the placement, ware patterns, and organization of places and things around them. Identifying "work-arounds," modifications, or innovations that may indicate problems or unmet needs can provide valuable insights leading to strategy innovations. For example, an architect or city planner might deliberately not build some or all of the necessary sidewalks around a building or in a certain public area and simply see where people choose to walk. Once the "natural" paths have been noted, the sidewalks can then be built where people actually want to walk. Unearthing people's expectations and values regarding speed, excitement, danger, and risk could have profound implications for industries such as air and automobile transportation (cf. Schiffer, 2004). At work, a large number of photos of peoples' family and/or friends in and around their workspaces might imply something important about their values, attitudes, and beliefs or their emotional connections to your industry, products, or services. Noting what people keep out in view versus what they put away in drawers and cabinets, what people do before they get ready to leave for the day or for a week's vacation, and where people spend their time can all lead to ideas for new strategy, products, services, business models, and industries.

> While designing the phone for Kyocera, I learned that teens had less interest in smoking when they owned a mobile device that supported gaming or texting. The social awkwardness of attending ones first college party as a freshman is as daunting now as it was in the 80's. My generation suppressed that anxiety by looking

cool with a cigarette while more of today's teens are choosing to look cool while texting (often their parents) on a mobile phone. This type of information must be sought out to be understood. (Frank, Industrial Designer)

While observing people there are scores of important questions that can be used to stimulate and deepen our creative thinking about user's needs and desires that can lead us to creative strategy innovations (adapted from Fulton Suri, 2005; Godin, 2001; Osborn, 1953):

Who
- Who is doing it?
- Who else is or could be doing this?
- Who else could do this easier or better and why?

What
- What else is or could be doing this?
- What should be or is being done?
- What is that? How is that being used?
- What are those people doing? What ideas does this suggest?
- What patterns are we seeing here?
- What is the underlying, universal need here?
- What is next to what? What does this go with? What happens before or after? This is smaller than what, or larger than what? What would cause this effect?
- What is this like? What attribute has this in common with that? How is this the same as that? What about the component parts?
- What is this not like? What is the point of difference? What about the opposite? Does the past offer a parallel?
- What situations might benefit from creative combinations of the objects we see here?
- What are the implied human relations and needs here, and how might we as an organization respond to these?
- What service/products opportunities are suggested here?
- What about...? What if...? What else?
- What other uses could this be put to? In what new ways could we use this?
- What else could be made from this?
- To what use can the "waste" be put? Who might be able to use it as it is or with some modifications?

- In what ways can we "invite" the customers/users to change their behavior to make the product/service work dramatically differently or better?
- What else could be adapted? Is there something similar I can legally "copy"? What can I make this look like? What idea can I incorporate?
- What would happen if I substituted this for that, move this over there?
- What other process could be used or adapted? What if there was more/less, bigger/smaller? What could I add? Can it be stronger, fatter, thinner, more/less frequent, heavier/lighter, and so on? What can we leave out?
- What things/ideas can be combined? What about a blend, an assortment, an ensemble?

Where
- Where is it being done or should it be done or could it be done?
- Where else is or could someone be doing this?
- Where else could this be placed/arranged? Can we transpose positive and negative? What about the opposite? Can we turn it over, make "up," be "down"?

How
- How thoughtless, spontaneous, or unconscious versus planned is the behavior?
- How can we change things that are completely functional/utilitarian and make them more meaningful, personal, exciting, beautiful, or decorative?
- How would I/they know that? What qualities have been recognized and exploited here?
- How/when is relevant information being provided where and when it is needed, in its natural sequence?
- How are people "productively" using their time here or are they "wasting" time?
- How/when are issues of privacy, crowding, and social distance relevant?
- How might an electronic version be an improvement?
- How can we add value via a "throwback" or a "retro" version?
- How can we make the experience more convenient, efficient, faster, enjoyable, entertaining, and/or safe?
- How should/could they do it? How could this be modified to fit a new use?

- How could you use your technology and expertise to make a better product/service for your customers'/users' standard behavior?
- How could we do this better or cheaper, safer or faster? How might this be altered, modified, changed?
- How can we make it simpler, reduce the number of parts? How can we double it/cut it in half?
- How else can this be arranged?

Why
- Why are they doing that? Why there? Is there something enjoyable about it?
- Why are they grouped like that? Why are they alone?
- Why is it that people apparently avoid being here?
- Why has someone placed this object here?
- Why is this necessary?
- Why do they seem happy, sad, angry, frustrated, and so on.?

When
- When is it being done/should it be done/could it be done?
- Does this have to happen before that?
- What if the order were changed?
- Are there time-of-year (i.e., seasonal) or time-of-day issues involved?
- How do people know when it is time or not time to do this?
- How many times does this need to be done and can we alter that?

Ask: Ask People to Help You by Collecting Relevant Information
The third set of qualitative research methods are really nontraditional variants of the more traditional interview and questionnaire methodologies. There are four methods we will discuss in this subsection.

Behavior sampling. Another method for collecting data about what people actually do, rather than what they think and say they do, is behavioral sampling. In this case, you give people a pager or mobile phone and ask them to record and evaluate the situation they are in when it rings at random times. This way, you get data about what people do that is less tainted by memory, expectations, or biases.

Extreme user interviews (also called "unfocus groups" by Nussbaum, 2004). Identify individuals who are extremely familiar (e.g., experts) or extremely unfamiliar (e.g., novices) or someone who has never heard of or tried your product, service, or industry and ask them to evaluate their experiences with it. This will give you insights from the two extremes instead of using averaged data. For the experts, your product, service, and industry may have become routine and you can see what happens as a result of repeated exposure or use. Alternatively, they may have figured out some shortcuts, aids, or improvements you can use. When people use your product, service, or industry for the first time, you may find out that you have made many assumptions and taken many things for granted that novices and first-time customers do not. They may do something or use something in a novel or unthought-of way, simply because they do not know any better. Again, this can provide valuable insights about latent needs and underlying functions and values that can lead to opportunities for strategy innovation. For example, collecting data about the average use of home entertainment technology leads to information such as the average teen plays ten hours of online video games per month or the average adult watches four hours of television per day, but is not going to give us new ideas for home entertainment strategy innovations. Knowing that the average person goes to a hospital 5.2 times a year or flies 3.3 times a year is not going to help us radically redesign the patient-hospital or travel experiences. On the other hand, interviewing first-time fliers or video game players, as well as long-term hospital patients, extremely frequent fliers or video game players, might give us insights into what they fear, what the experience means to them, what they value, what they aspire to, and what they like and dislike about the alternatives with which they are familiar. All of this could lead to ideas for significant strategy innovations.

Draw the experience. Instead of interviewing people about their experiences, ask them to think about and visualize an experience or interaction with your product or service, and then draw a picture or diagram of it. This drawing can be literal or symbolic. This might give you insights into how positive or negative the emotions are that are associated with the experience. You might get a sense of what your customers think and feel are the most salient elements of their experiences. You might get an insight into how the customer perceived their experiences differently than you do. A variation of this method is a camera journal. In this case you give some customers a camera and ask them to keep visual diaries of their activities and impressions related to your products and services, company or industry.

Ask "Why?" or "So what?" five times. Another way to get your customers or clients to provide you directly with useful information is to ask a series of probing questions. Ask five "Why?" or "So what?" questions in response to five consecutive answers. This process helps you to get to the core or the underlying issue, problem or value.

> You just need to keep asking the questions, "So what? What does that mean?"
> Question—"If you get the expected extra $50 per tonne what does that mean?"
> Answer—"Well, that means our return on capital breaks our investment threshold."
> Question—"So, why do care about that?"
> Answer—"Because we believe we have to grow massively in scale in order to survive. In order to grow we need funds. Those funds have to come from investors. Investors use a threshold return criteria to determine who they are willing to give funds to."
> Question—"So at the heart of this you need more money from your investors?"
> Answer—"Yes."

We now know that is the core issue. We now know we need to investigate whether there is anything in the investor–company relationship that was open to influence. Why go through the painstaking process of making more money in order to persuade someone to give you more capital if there is a shot at getting them to just give you the capital. Given the amount of effort and time at stake, while it may be embarrassing, it is not stupid to just ask them for more money. It may or may not produce the results but you would be stupid not to turn over that stone. (Andrew, Designer, Management Consultant)

Try: Create Prototypes and Simulations to
Help You Empathize with Customers

The final set of nontraditional, qualitative research methods involves building models, simulations, and/or prototypes that can be used to help you empathize with customers, and help you evaluate and refine your solutions. While there is truly "nothing like the real thing," models, simulations, and/or prototypes can help us get as close as possible, quickly and efficiently. We will discuss these methods in more detail later in chapter five and then again more briefly in chapters six and seven, as models and prototyping are core elements of any design process. Here, we will look briefly at two ways to use prototypes and simulations to help us gain insights into our customers' experiences and mindsets to enable us to gather data that will be useful when trying to generate strategy innovations.

Once again, the idea with these methods is to generate data, information, and knowledge from direct experience, rather than from traditional surveys, questionnaires, market analysis, or technical reports. Instead of observing and/or asking your customers for second-hand information and impressions, with these methods the impressions, information, and knowledge are generated directly from clients/customers, and experienced first-hand by those responsible for decision-making, problem-solution, or strategy development as they try out prototypes and simulations for themselves.

Be your customer. Describe, outline, or enact a typical customer experience. Try mock journeys in which the experience of a customer or target person is simulated or actually taken. Few airline executives are likely to regularly fly economy-class. If they wanted to know what the majority of their customers experienced, they should fly economy-class or stand-by from New York to Sydney or from London to Beijing. If a doctor or hospital administrator wanted to redesign the health care experience, they should check themselves into their own clinics or hospitals anonymously. University administrators should enroll, sign-up for, and take a class at their own and other universities. Real estate agents should go anonymously to a partner or another agency and try to buy a house. City mayors, administrators, and counselors should ride the bus to and from work for a year.

Informance. Act out an "informative performance" (i.e., an informance) by play acting roles, insights, or behaviors that you have witnessed or researched. One of the best ways to empathize with someone and to gain insight into how they are thinking and feeling is to do what they do literally. On an emotional level, if you want to know what someone is thinking and feeling (but you cannot or do not want to ask them) as they walk around with their heads down, hands in pockets, and with their back hunched-over, the best thing for you to do is to adopt their physiology for five or ten minutes and sense how you feel. It is by no means a perfect method, but it is better than most others I have tried.

An excellent example of this comes from the work of Catenazzo and Fragniere (2009). They wanted to know if an up-service repositioning of travel agents from booking agents simply selling airline tickets to travel consultants providing a knowledge-based service was a viable strategy or was a more radical reinvention of the industry needed? They conducted two theater-based experiments (i.e., infor-mances) to investigate. One informance was of a low-quality service experience and one of a high-quality experience. They had two dif-ferent groups of independent observers watch the informances then state their willingness to pay, and price the service experiences from the customers' perspective. They also calculated the break-even point for a travel agent's services and assumed "that the value of a service experience perceived by clients must be far higher than its production costs to ensure the economical sustainability of the service" (p. 10). Their analyses illustrated that two-thirds of respondents' willingness-to-pay was below the required break-even point. This led them to the conclusion that a simple repositioning of travel agents to travel consultants was not a viable option as too few people were willing to pay enough for the service experience to make such a business sus-tainable. Of course, the next, and likely infinitely more valuable set of insights, must be discovering what customers do value enough to pay a premium for.

Interpreting Qualitative Data

While the first step in the qualitative research process is collecting good data, the second, more difficult step is interpreting it. Anyone can collect observations, draw maps, take pictures and videos, and talk to customers. The real value comes from the ability to interpret the information, derive meaning from it, recognize patterns, latent needs, underlying functions, values, opportunities, and implications, and then to generate ideas for strategy innovation. Several authors (Gummesson, 2000; Jirotka and Luff, 2006; Reese, 2004; Ulrich and Eppinger, 2004) have reminded us that interpreting the qualitative data we have collected is the key to business success and it is not often an easy or straightforward process.

There are many things to keep in mind when trying to interpret qualitative data. First, we must remember that traditional quantita-tive research methods used for strategy and marketing data collection have been developed and are used "based on the belief that observers are independent and that science is value-free...relates to the facts or causes of social phenomena and attempts to explain causal relation-ships by means of objective facts" (Carson et al., 2001, p. 5). There is little need for interpretation of quantitative data as it is concerned with objective facts, rational description, and the identification of the numerically optimal right or best answer.

Qualitative data collection methods, on the other hand, have been developed and are used to focus "on understanding what is happening in a given context. It includes consideration of multiple realities, different actors' perspectives, researcher involvement, taking account of the contexts of the phenomena under study, and the contextual understanding and interpretation of data" (ibid.). By definition, when dealing with qualitative data the goal is to try and understand what is happening, to consider multiple options and perspectives, and to become involved. The goal is not to stay separate and objective trying to reveal the one right answer that exists in the data but to interpret the meanings and emotional connections that may be there below the surface and to gain insights into situations, phenomena, problems, and their potential solutions. This interpretation requires creativity and insight, balanced with discipline and effort, with some educated guesswork most likely thrown in as well.

This does not mean, however, that "anything goes" when trying to interpret qualitative data. We still must be concerned with making sure both our data and the conclusions we draw from them are as legitimate (i.e., reliable and valid) as possible. Toward this end, there are several things we can do. The first is to try and make whatever we do as transparent as possible by documenting everything that is done, and by listing the assumptions we make when reaching a conclusion or making an interpretation.

A good way to increase transparency is to develop explicit criteria for analysis. The criteria used for interpretations or evaluation should be clear, relevant, and comprehensive, and based on the research purpose, goals, and objectives, and any literature reviews conducted.

Transparency is needed most in the interpretation of findings, with clear descriptions and explanations of why a given interpretation is made. The validity of this transparency can be strengthened by linking the interpretation to prior theory and to any conceptual theory building in a study. Transparency is a vital dimension in the value of interpretive qualitative research methodologies. (p. 69)

Hearn (2006) provided a good example of how explicit evaluation criteria can be used to improve the quality of a qualitative analysis. Hearn (2006) discussed the evaluation of the quality of banking websites. Several independent evaluators were asked to rate the bank's websites on their content, page layout, navigational ease, formatting, interactivity, help functions, security, and overall performance. While the speed of the web pages loading could have been measured objectively, all other criteria were subjective. By making the criteria explicit, by providing a rating scheme (e.g., very poor, poor, average, good, very good), and by using multiple raters, the qualitative assessment became more transparent, reliable, and valid.

In addition to increasing the transparency of our methods and interpretations, which will increase their reliability, we can do several things to try and increase both their reliability and validity. There are many software tools that can help with data content analysis and data coding (cf. Bazeley, 2003; Carson et al., 2001). Simply counting the frequency of key words, concepts, or ideas, or creating categories and sorting answers into the best fitting category can help increase reliability and validity as opposed to simply relying on a few statements that stand out in our memory or other anecdotal evidence. This conversion of qualitative data into numerical codes that can be represented statistically is well researched and documented and is referred to as "quantizing" data (cf. Tashakkori and Teddlie, 2003).

As mentioned earlier in relation to pattern recognition, triangulation or getting data or interpretations from multiple sources also increases our confidence in them. When trying to interpret data or establish the meaning of something, using three or more "raters" or "interpreters" improves the quality of our interpretation. "Used in navigation, land survey, and civil engineering, [the term] triangulation is used for the application of two or more methods on the same research problem to increase the reliability of the results" (Gummesson, 2000, p. 142). For example, if you get data from your observations and from several other sources all pointing in the same direction, you would be more confident in it than if you based your conclusions solely on your observations. When trying to interpret the meaning of a symbol or activity, using multiple raters and interpreters increases our confidence in the reliability and validity of our interpretation. Studying the same topic over a long period of time has a similar effect. Finally, whenever possible, if we use both qualitative and quantitative data collections methods, or if we use explicitly designed mixed research methods (cf. Tashakkori and Teddlie, 2003), these multiple methods should also increase the quality of our research efforts. All these techniques make the research and interpretation process more transparent to others, more repeatable by others (i.e., more reliable), and of higher quality (i.e., more valid; Johnson and Turner, 2003).

When we judge their ability to make jewellery, it is purely technical and clinical regarding its manufacture. [Objective assessment]

Design is always more personal; is there visual symmetry, is the piece balanced, is there a focal point, did they make something stand out, are there smooth flowing lines, is it functional and practical? Because this is subjective, with competitions we always have multiple judges. [Subjective assessment with triangulation] (Dave, Fine Jeweller)

When working with qualitative data, we should also try to collect small amounts of data at one time and try to make sense of them, before collecting too much more. "Collect a small amount of initial data, develop preliminary analyses, and use these to focus the next data-collection activity" (Jirotka and Luff, 2006, p. 44). This iterative process allows us to learn as we go and helps ensure we will be collecting useful data. Recall the hallmark of a designerly way of knowing discussed in chapter two related to the brief. The key was to have a design attitude that was solution focused, willing to iteratively explore, search, try, and learn, as opposed to a problem focused attitude that was concerned with choosing quickly the one best or right answer from among the given alternatives. The analysis and interpretation of qualitative data is an iterative process of exploration and learning, not a rigid, hierarchical, mechanistic process of calculating the best or single right answer.

When interpreting qualitative data, it is also important to try and think holistically. An essential part of the designerly way of thinking is the ability to "oscillate" attention (Cross, Dorst, and Roozenburg, 1992). When we interpret qualitative data we must think holistically and iterate (or oscillate attention) between understanding the problem and formulating a solution, between thinking (e.g., analysis) and doing (e.g., prototyping), and continually be willing to change back and forth between rational, left-brain thinking[5] (i.e., an analytical, logical, and sequential approach to problem framing and solving) and nonrational, right-brain thinking (i.e., an intuitive, values-based, and nonlinear approach). Left-brain thinkers usually proceed in linear, sequential, logical steps (Cross, 2000). They try to get everything clear before moving on. On the other hand, more intuitive right-brain thinkers proceed more broadly, gathering information from a range of areas. Successful qualitative data interpretation is essentially a holistic process requiring both left-brain and right-brain thinking. If you usually think like a scientist, in order to successfully interpret qualitative data you need some of the artist's divergent thinking to perceive new possibilities. If you usually think like an artist, you need some of the scientist's single-minded perseverance to help you focus (Lawson, 2004).

This requirement for holism is one of the reasons qualitative data interpretation is so difficult. It is also one of the reasons why if you can do it, it will lead to strategy innovation and success (cf. Mockler, 2006). If we can engage our thinking hearts and feeling minds, and balance creativity with profit, a left-brain approach with a right-brain approach, our Yin with Yang, the innovative/creative with the cost focused, the frivolous with the pragmatic, intuition with reason, our "book smarts" with our "street smarts," and the mechanistic with the organic, we will wind up with products, services, strategies, and industries that are unique and achievable, value adding to people and society on the one hand while making money for us and our organizations on the other. These are the goals of strategy innovation by design.

Another key to successful qualitative data interpretation is to focus on what is happening and why from the perspective of the subject, not from our personal or organizational perspective. We will be more likely to successfully interpret qualitative data if we are able to empathize and be as free as possible from our existing biases, assumptions, and paradigms through our focus on action (i.e., verbs) rather than things (i.e., nouns) as discussed in chapter two. We will be more likely to successfully interpret qualitative data and find underlying values and latent needs if we focus on peoples' activities and experiences and shift from thinking about our preconceived notions of objects (i.e., nouns) to thinking about the actions, functions, and behavior (i.e., verbs) we have identified through our research (Fulton Suri, 2005; Ulrich and Eppinger, 2004). To help us uncover the meaning in the data we have collected, we must look for the underlying values and the emotional connections underlying the experience. We must focus on what is actually happening, and we must interpret and speculate to try and understand why it is happening from the subjects' or customers' point of view. This will help us to identify the latent needs our products, services, organizations, and industries can then fulfil with strategy innovation.

It is also important not to ignore any activities, artifacts, or situations just because they seem inconsequential to the subject or unimportant to you at first. Just because they are not important to you does not mean they are not important to the subjects. Similarly, just because the subjects do not seem to explicitly recognize the importance of something does not mean it is not important to them. A significant proportion of our knowledge is tacit. Many of our unconscious habits and much of our intuitive expertise

> represents know-how that has been built and honed often through years of experience. But often it has also become so deeply embedded that it is not immediately apparent, even to those who possess it... [when we] notice and document their habits, workarounds, unspoken rules, and cryptic signalling systems, we can work together to uncover the opportunities for improvement. Then we can also evaluate and refine new ideas and prototypes with a sharper awareness of the realities of the living context. (Fulton Suri, 2005, pp. 175–176)

Finally, looking for metaphors, archetypes, or stories (Lajocono and Zaccai, 2004) can help us make sense of our qualitative data. A good metaphor or analogy can help us understand a situation by giving us a frame of reference with which we are familiar. Personifying the typical consumer or articulating the archetypical situation can similarly help us by giving us something to visualize. We have been thinking and communicating in stories for millennia. Finding coherent or semi-coherent stories and scenarios in our qualitative data can help us make sense of what we are seeing by helping us to link elements, and explore motives and underlying meaning, emotions and values.

CHAPTER FOUR

Concept Generation: The Art (and Science) of Generating Different Views

Once they have defined the problem, developed a brief, and conducted various forms of research to gain insights into related aspects of the customer and the problem, designers tend to use all of the information and insights gained to generate concepts and ideas to start to develop potential solutions. "The emphasis at this stage is on a wider, intuitive type of thinking in which lateral thinking, exploring many possibilities, rather than vertical thinking, concentrating on a single line of reasoning, is of great value" (Sowrey, 1987, p. 17). During this concept generation phase a number of alternative approaches and concepts are created and explored. Later a smaller number are prototyped (chapter five) and evaluated (chapter six) as part of a developmental cycle. We will focus in this chapter on the idea generation process from a design perspective, as there are many other works that address the topic of creativity more broadly.

Ideation: Concept Generation via Hard Work and Incubation

In the design world, there seem to be two stories about where concepts and ideas come from. The first story has to do with intuition, inspiration, incubation, illumination, and a divine spark or insight. This is the more romantic view of the creative process.

I choose the time of day to work, high energy, before daybreak. (Richard, Landscape Architect)

I try and do nothing. I get in a rhythm and a flow. I sleep. I do not want to force it, no rush, not to think about it too much. (Frank, Graphic Designer)

The second view suggests that the generative process is hard work. It takes time, effort, and the application of various skills and techniques to yield creative solutions and innovative thinking.

I work, I draw and I change modes. (Karen, Architect)

When I am stuck for an idea I look at other art. Even if it's entirely unrelated, seeing other artistic projects, in virtually any media, always gets the juices flowing. (Troy, Graphic Designer and Illustrator)

I read the literature. (Colin, Graphic Designer)

Ideation is done via reading and then visualizing. I am always looking for new visual experiences and reading information and looking for new physical experiences to gain insight. (Charles, Architect)

DeBono-related techniques are good like brainstorming, but also self-awareness. You have to know your natural mode of thinking and then deliberately flip that around to be creative. (Todd, Interior Designer, Design Educator)

I suggest it is not one story or the other that is true about concept generation, but as with many things, it is a bit of both stories that forms the truth. Several designers also seemed to agree.

How much of creativity is hard work versus unconscious inspiration varies depending upon the stage in the process. Early on it is more creative than later into production where it becomes more hard work. (Diana, Graphic Designer)

Creativity is 5% inspiration and 95% perspiration. I encourage students to work hard, do their research and that way gain confidence in their ability. (Robert, Multimedia and Web Designer, Design Educator)

Creativity starts with inspiration. Without the inspiration there is no perspiration. You get the concept at the start and perspire later. (Lynda, Graphic Designer, Book Designer)

Courageousness is important in creativity. You must be able to explore without boundaries things like feeling and mood to create something new. With no fear this can come whenever it is required. Creativity is an active choice that comes from knowledge and skill. The artist who relies on doing many things and picking the one that is good is simply showing their lack of training. A clear understanding of skills is critical. Knowledge and skills and how to combine culture and emotions, it's deeper than just technology. (Simon, 3-D Animator, Master Jeweller)

An example in practice of this combination of technique and hard work, along with letting go to allow intuition and insight to have an effect, happened twice to me while writing this book. The first paragraph of the first chapter "jumped" into my mind fully formed at about three o'clock one morning (i.e., inspiration) after having thought, discussed, worked, read, and tried everything for weeks (i.e., perspiration) to succinctly and simply articulate the main thesis of this work and how it related to the more traditional strategy development process. After significant effort and struggle, I gave up and stopped thinking and worrying about it. I continued to work on other aspects of the book and eventually, the answer came to me. The same thing happened when I wrote the last paragraph of the first chapter about the iterative and repetitive nature of many elements of the design process. I had thought several times over a period of weeks that I was repeating myself while writing. For example, I would read and edit the chapter on evaluation, and then on the next day while working on the chapter related to the brief I felt I was saying something alarmingly similar. I then went back to the evaluation chapter to check and see if I was repeating myself. I was not literally repeating my self but was discussing something similar from a different perspective. I had done this five times during a three-week period (i.e., hard work). I had gone back through every chapter looking for repetition and could not find any. Eventually, I decided to let it be for a while and see what happened (i.e., incubation). Then at 2 a.m. one morning I woke up with that paragraph on my lips. I got out of bed, wrote it down, and went back to sleep.

In order to be truly creative and to use this to generate strategy innovations, therefore, we must work hard, apply the techniques and the skills we have, and at some appropriate point, give it a rest, take a break, and allow unconscious processes to incubate and provide us with

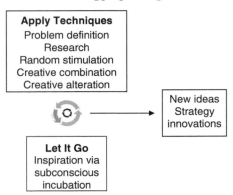

Figure 4.1   Ideation via hard work and incubation.

inspiration, new perspectives, and insights, before beginning to work at it again as illustrated in figure 4.1. We will, therefore, discuss aspects of both of these sides of the ideation and concept generation story in the remainder of this chapter.

Generating a Different View

Regardless of which perspective makes most sense to them (i.e., hard work, incubation, or some of both), many designers seem to agree that concept generation is a critical part of the design process, and that its purpose is to generate a different view.

> Definitely conceptualising is the most difficult part of the pro-cess...coming up with the concepts is always the hardest thing, the thing that strings all the needs and wants together and the functionalities of design together. It's not just something that looks pretty. That is often the most painstaking thing to put together and sometimes the easiest, depending on if you're on a good design day or a bad design day. (Julia, Architect)

> The creative stage, the initial conceptual ideas stage, is the most important because that is the stage where you have the most flexibility. (Brad, Museum Design Manager)

> Creativity is seeing from a different perspective. (Kay, Interior Designer)

Of course, when trying to generate organizational strategy in practice, strategists sometimes use creativity techniques. There are a plethora of interesting and helpful books (cf. Bilton, 2007; Florida, 2002; Rickards, 1989; Sauber, 2006) and research articles (cf. Beaver, 2001; Mockler, 2006; Robins, 1960) that have been, and continue to be, published related to creativity and idea generation for strategy and business. Designers, however, have a few techniques and practices that they seem to find uniquely valuable and these are important for strategy innovation development.

Quantity over Quality at First: Generate Many Concepts and Ideas

One thing strategy developers can learn from designers regarding idea generation is that success comes from generating a diverse range of concepts and ideas, not from focusing on developing the "right one." Designers and people studying creativity have known for years that the secret to successful solution generation is to focus on quantity over quality at first (Godin, 2005; Osborn, 1953; Rickards, 1992; Russo, 2006; Sawyer, 2006; Schrage, 2000). Also related to this concept of quantity over quality of ideas is the well-known notion that "mistakes sometimes turn into lucky accidents" (Osborn, 1953, p. 207).

According to Altier (1988), "The value of failure was recognised by IBM's Thomas J. Watson when he said, 'The way to succeed is to double your failure rate' " (p. 159). Quantity of ideas maximizes the chance of obtaining the best solution while minimizing early commitment to an inadequate solution. This is critical. Problem solution is often a numbers game and there must be many experiments, trials, models, and failures along the road to success. Unfortunately, the data suggest that when we try to solve problems we tend to become focused on initial ideas and rarely generate, model, and consider alternatives (cf. Ball, Ormerod, and Maskill, 1997). This is especially relevant for strategy innovators as our rational, problem-focused thinking and research methods tend to focus us on finding the one right answer quickly.

Techniques for Generating Many Concepts and Ideas

There are many techniques that designers use to help them generate concepts. The first and foremost technique has to do with combining ideas. Creative combination or creative alteration has been discussed for decades by both researchers and practitioners (Altier, 1988; Evans, 1991; Godin, 2005; Kelley, 2005; Kim, 1990; Kim and Mauborgne, 1999; Osborn, 1953; Russo, 2006). In many ways it is true that there is nothing new under the sun. Many new ideas are unique combinations of other ideas. Other idea generation techniques we will discuss are adjusting the physical work environment, random stimulation, identifying and questioning assumptions, emotional expression and release, and incubation.

Creative Combination and Alteration

To come up with something new, we sometimes have to make use of what is already available. Quite frequently we can see that it is the creative combination of two or more previously unrelated aspects that eventually leads to a value breakthrough. For example, combining two existing ideas, applying something that works in one area to another area, reversing direction whenever a direction is implied, reversing a relationship whenever there is a relationship implied, and denying things that are taken for granted are all tried and true means of generating a number of new ideas.

Two of the designers interviewed (Catroina and Garth, architects) related the story of what happened when they were part of a group of people working for the Public Rail Authority in Sydney, Australia, trying to solve a problem. There had been an alarming increase in the number of instances of people throwing things off of overpasses and hitting moving trains. If a train driver traveling at high speed gets hit by a rock thrown from an overpass it can be a disaster. The problem-solving group members were thinking of all sorts of ways to put up screens, barriers, and defenses to keep people from being able to throw things off overpasses down onto trains. Everything they thought of was either not doable or exceedingly expensive given the number and size of the overpasses with which they had to deal. The value of creative combination and alteration was illustrated when someone turned their thinking around and said, "Instead of putting barriers up to try and keep people from throwing things off of overpasses, let's turn the problem around and protect the drivers by putting front window barriers up on each train engine." In the end, they decided to put a small screen in front of each train's windshield to protect the drivers. While this seems obvious and simple when written out like this, when you are focused on trying to find ways to keep people from throwing things off of overpasses, it is not an obvious solution until you deliberately apply the technique of reversing directions/relationships.

> Creativity is seeing things upside down. (Kay, Interior Designer)

> Creativity is from outside of the box, putting concepts together in a unique and inspiring way. (Richard, Graphic and Digital Multimedia Designer)

> Creativity is a visualization process of sketching, doodling and applying trigger words to get you down a different path. (Todd, Interior Designer, Design Educator)

Another example of creative combination comes from King Island in the Bass Strait, the bit of sea separating Tasmania from the south of the Australian mainland:

> King Island has two problems, a future shortage of wood and mountains of cardboard. Now a joint effort between its main industries—kelp and dairy—has seen the two problems merge and a possible solution take shape...Briquettes made from cardboard waste from King Island Dairy will help fuel the island's kelp drying kilns...Both sides win; the dairy gets rid of its waste and the kilns have the prospect of cheaper fuel. (Neals, 2006)

Other, more well-known historical examples of creative combination and alteration are:

- Dell who altered catalogue and online shopping, and combined that model with PC sales.
- Chrysler who combined the best of the car and the van to create the now ubiquitous minivan.
- Cirque du Soleil who combined circus and theater.
- "Healthy" has been combined with "fast foods" and this has lead to World Wrapps, O'Naturals, Healthy Bites, Mr. Goodburger's, Tops, Chick-fil-A, Jamba Juice, Au Bon Pain, and a resurgence of Subway.

The ability to associate and combine ideas in novel and unexpected ways is the essence of creativity. "Creativity is the ability to discover new relationships, to look at subjects from new perspectives, and to form new combinations from two or more concepts already in the mind" (Evans, 1991, p. 71).

> I get inspiration from words as well as other imagery. Words create the basis for the ideas. For example ... A music venue called Music Uptown. What visuals can exemplify this? I think of the words "up" and the idea of "direction." This leads me to compasses, maps, sky, triangles (part of an arrow). While glancing through magazines, art books, photography and illustration books and websites I find clouds. The image on the cover becomes a cloud shaped like a music note, the name of the venue becomes typeset into a triangle pointing up. Another version becomes a stylized compass with north being repeated inside the brochure. Secondary elements are solid and dotted lines creating [musical] movement, and music staff lines. (Lynn, Graphic Designer)

The roles of the cross-pollinator, who explores many industries and cultures then translates the insights and revelations gained and applies them to a new problem, and the collaborator, who helps link different groups together and helps create new combinations and multi-disciplinary solutions, have been recognized and discussed by Kelley (2005, pp. 8–11). These are innovation roles specifically focused on using creative combination to generate ideas for new products and services. I am suggesting they also need to be applied to the creative combination of ideas for strategy innovation, new industries, and business models, and to the solution of our most intractable social and financial problems.

In terms of how you actually generate ideas through creative combination, Altier (1988) suggested the first step is to forget everything you know about existing relationships and the way things work now. The second step is to remember everything you know about the individual pieces involved. The third step is to rearrange everything you know about the pieces by putting them into new relationships. (See table 4.1 for a listing of creative combination and alteration trigger questions I compiled from many sources over the course of writing this book.) Altier talked about this in terms of Pablo Picasso's statement that "every act of creation is first of all an act of destruction." We must destroy what we know and assume about the existing relationships between ideas and the way things work currently, as this frees us up to

Table 4.1 Creative combination and alteration questions

Assumptions	*Increase*
What is given and assumed? How can I violate these assumptions?	What can I increase, add, repeat, transfer, animate, extend, develop, magnify, expand, make bigger, longer, heavier, funnier, sadder, more extreme, open, and so on?
Combine	
What can I add to this?	
What ideas can I combine, connect, attach, put together, superimpose, integrate, link, mix, merge, synthesize with this?	*Minimize*
What purposes, values or ideals can I combine, integrate, link, synthesize, and so on?	What can I reduce, break down, decrease, make smaller, shorter, lighter, close, and so on?
	What can I take away, condense, split, break?
Apply in a new area	
What works in other areas that might work here?	*Substitute*
What do I like to do that can be applied here?	Who, what, how, where, why, when else can we or others do this?
How can what I am or we are good at be applied in other areas?	Can I copy this or something else (legally)?
	Can I replace this or use this to replace something?
Change	What else can this be used for?
How can I change the direction, timing, relationship, color, feel, smell, taste, shape, meaning, form, material, texture, context?	How can we stop, block, or replace this?
Can I provide choice, flexibility, movement, activity, fun, power, spirit, heart?	*Reversing*
	Can I reverse the direction?
	Can I reverse the relationship?
What can I infer, refer, reflect, construct, reconstruct, break, fragment, isolate, distort, highlight?	What can I reverse, turn inside-out, upside down, left-side right, oppose, resist, contradict, parody, and so on?

think about things in new ways, and then rearrange things into completely new relationships.

I also break things down and dream and fantasize, play and sensualize, juxtapose and see something new to be creative. Creativity is deconstruction, breaking it down. (Rod, Illustrator and Design Educator)

Creativity is breaking it down into smaller bits. (Kay, Interior Designer)

While this sounds good, and we know that it works, it is easier said then done. One way to make this happen is to bring in outsiders. Kim

(1990), who also thinks that forgetting what we know and looking for new relationships are keys to creativity, suggested,

> Ignorance is power when it gives the novice courage to push ahead where experts fear to tread. The newcomer, bringing fresh insight and bearing no prejudice against what cannot be accomplished, transforms the impossible into possible... Almost by definition, creativity does not reside in the identification of familiar relationships among familiar objects. (p. 12)

Similarly, consider the following from Sawyer (Russo, 2006),

> here's where we come up against another of our cultural myths about creativity—that of the lone genius. Ideas don't magically appear in the genius' head from nowhere. They always build on what came before. And collaboration is key. Look at what others in your field are doing. Brainstorm with people in different fields. Research and anecdotal evidence suggests that distant analogies lead to new ideas—like when a heart surgeon bounces things off an architect or a graphic designer. (p. 90)

When was the last time you invited an outsider or a novice into your strategy development process? Instead, you are more likely to have restricted the participation to the experts and a privileged few.

Another example of creative combination is how I came up with the idea to write this book. I regularly read a great deal both in my areas of expertise and from outside it. Every month I read books, magazine articles, refereed journal publications, newspaper articles, Internet blogs, and so on. During one period of time I noticed a pattern: three or four people were writing about the importance of design to organizations. These authors were saying that design thinking should come out of the product development area and into our thinking about organizations more broadly. I thought this made great sense. I had never before made the connection between design (designing buildings or products) and designing systems and organizations. I started to think about the possibility that if someone is skilled at designing chairs, shavers, advertising, jewellery, houses, and the like, maybe we could learn something from them about how to design our organizations better. This was an example of the creative combination of ideas. I started to think about how new product design might be like organizational design. Unfortunately, the more I thought about this, it seemed as though it actually did not make sense to me. The design or structure of an organization is not easy for me to conceive of in the way I conceive of designing a physical structure or artifact. So, I dropped the idea for a while. This was an example of incubation. I let go of the idea for a while and kept it in the "back of my mind." A few days later, I was preparing a lecture on how to implement strategy, when the thought struck me that maybe we could apply what we know about great design in products and homes to the design of strategy rather than the structure of organizations. The more I thought about this, the more it did make sense. This creatively combining and connecting ideas (organizational strategy design and development with the design profession) started me down the path of writing this book.

Kim and Mauborgne (1999) have provided several suggestions relevant to this idea of creative combination and alteration applied to strategy innovation:

1. Instead of focusing on trying to compete with rivals within your own industry, they suggested some creative alteration could lead you to look across to related substitute industries. For example, if you are in the movie industry, do not try and compete just with rival movie companies. Realize that you are within the broader entertainment industry and try to compete with related entertainment substitutes, such as television, the theater, and going out to dinner. In other words, you can innovate strategically and grow not simply by taking market share away from your direct competitors, but by creating new market spaces as Cirque du Soleil did or by taking market share away from related substitute industries. Another example is Southwest Airlines who altered its thinking and stopped acting as if other airlines were its competitors. "Southwest reasoned that for short-haul destinations, the automobile was a substitute for flying...it focused on why people fly (to save time) and why people drive (to save money)" Mockler (2006, p. 2). They took market share, not from other airlines, but from the untapped market of drivers who would fly if the price was right.

2. Instead of focusing on competitive position within your strategic group, they suggested looking across strategic groups to other strategic positions for opportunities. In other words, if you are competing within the high price, high-value position, look for a way to strategically innovate and gain some market share from companies positioned at the low price, low value position. For example,

supermarkets, universities, and departments stores that compete at the high-end of quality and service should explore some ways to try and compete with high-volume, lower-priced competitors. The supermarkets could produce their own generic brands as many already do. The universities could create a new brand and slash prices by offering an online or open-learning degree. The high-end department store could offer a money back lowest price guarantee while making sure its product ranges were as exclusive as possible to minimize head-to-head price competition.

3. Instead of focusing on how to better serve your existing customers, they suggested looking across the chain of buyers and altering your definition of who your customers actually are. They suggested that "In most industries, competitors converge around a common definition of who the target customer is when in reality there is a chain of 'customers' who are directly or indirectly involved in the buying decision" (Kim and Mauborgne, 1999, p. 87). Once you have more broadly defined who your customers are you might find that different customers have different perceptions of value that you have been overlooking. This could provide an opportunity for strategy innovation across various service levels or niches, for example.

4. Instead of focusing on trying to maximize the value of your product/service offerings within the bounds of your existing industry, they suggested looking across to complementary products/services that go beyond the bounds of your existing industry. For example, people in the entertainment industry, are actually affected by the ease and cost of a customer getting a babysitter and parking their car. My local movie theater has obviously learned this lesson as it offers free valet parking on Friday and Saturday nights and it offers special sessions on certain weekdays of first run movies for "babies and their carers."

5. Instead of focusing on trying to gain competitive advantage in line with the functional-emotional orientation of your existing industry, they suggested rethinking the functional-emotional orientation of your industry. If, for example, you are in a commodity industry and are competing based on price and function, they suggested trying to transform your functional product into an emotional, specially branded experience as Starbucks transformed coffee from a commodity (the routine drink, "marked by heavy price cutting and an ongoing battle for market share") into a relaxing, creative, social experience (Kim and Mauborgne,

1999, p. 90). All "generic" commodity products create new market space by shifting in the opposite direction. Generics remove the "specialness," the experience factor and the emotional brand appeal and can significantly reduce costs by shifting to a functional appeal. It can work in either direction.

Finally, consider this example illustrating the creative combination of what is typically thought of as theater and what is typically thought of as a museum exhibit:

> The exhibition at the Power House Museum [in Sydney Australia] for the Sydney 2000 Olympic Games on the original Olympic antiquities from Athens, was rewarding because Greece has never loaned these things to anybody anywhere else in the world. We ask them to lend us their prize treasures and antiquities from where the Olympic Games actually began. Because of the very strong Greek cultural community here in Australia we were able to get that approval to bring this material to Australia. We knew this was unusual and we wanted something special for our way to present the material here for the Sydney 2000 Olympic Games. We engaged a theatrical designer to work with our design team. So it was designed as a theatrical dramatic experience... from the time you arrived at the front entry there was this "genuine imitation" stone column rising up before you, and you walked up the ramp in the shadow of the column and as you stepped into the building you walked into a room with the voice of Zeus telling you about the exhibition you're about to experience. The fact that we engaged and linked drama and a different sort of creativity with the exhibition design creativity made it a very exciting design experience. And the response we got from visitors was overwhelmingly positive because of that. (Brad, Museum Design Manager)

The Physical Work Environment

A second technique for stimulating creativity, popular with designers, is to pay attention to the physical environment. The physical environment's impacts on our behavior, attitudes, and creativity have been well documented and noted for many years (Borghini, 2005; Carlopio, 1994; Carlopio and Gardner, 1992; Ceylan, Dul, and Aytac, 2008; Gibb and Waight, 2005; Rice, 1977; Vithayathawornwong, Danko, and Tolbert,

2008). In fact Kelly (2005) suggested that to be more creative we should act as directors and set designers to first gather together a talented cast and crew, and then help spark their creative talents by creating a stage on which innovation team members can do their best work, transforming physical environments into powerful tools to influence behavior and attitudes.

I am always looking for new physical experiences to help gain insights. (Charles, Architect)

It is not the most important thing but you do need access to information in the library and a place to get your hands dirty. (Rod, Illustrator and Design Educator)

It is important to work in a beautiful space. (Kay, Interior Designer)

Ideation is done using observation, being aware of what is around you. (Jorge, Design Educator)

I remember hearing or reading a story about how an architectural firm had a room maintained by someone so that it was always full of random and interesting things such as bits and pieces of many types of materials, novel shapes, toys, cornices, broken and working devices and technology, off-cuts, magazines, games, puzzles, and more. The value of the room was that the architects could go in there, look around, experiment, play, and get ideas and inspiration from the random collection of stuff and junk in the room.

Weinstein (2006) outlined the "four Ps" of physical environment-types that are needed to stimulate creativity: personal space, partnership space, public space, and personal computer (PC) space. Personal spaces provide storage space, comfort, and a safe creative bubble of privacy. They allow people to relax and concentrate when needed. Partnership spaces allow collaboration. As we discussed in chapter two, a diversity of inputs is an important contributor to successful decision-making, innovation, and creativity (cf. Prichard and Stanton, 1999; Yu, 2006). Public spaces also contribute to diversity and can stimulate our thinking by opening us up to different stimulus. Both formal and informal meetings can take place in partnership and public areas and they are designed in contrast to quiet, private spaces (Steiner, 2005). Finally, PC spaces are important to connect us to the unimaginable array of information and stimulation that various databases, search engines, software, and technology can provide.

Along with all of these flexible office-based physical work environments, it is important to remember that sometimes the best work space to stimulate creativity is not a traditional office environment at all. Given the technology available today, there is good reason to consider working from home, the beach, the mountains, and so on.

My inspiration often comes from nature, flora and fauna. I see ideas in my head from looking at a doorway, the side of the building, a nut or a bolt. My designs normally come from a shape I have seen. (Dave, Fine Jeweller)

Many of us are at our most creative when we are not in office environments at all.

Random Stimulation

A third technique for stimulating creativity is to seek random stimulation. This can come in a number of forms such as (1) exposing yourself to the out-of-the-ordinary in terms of travel; (2) seeking out information, media, and people from industries other than your own and from outside your area of expertise; (3) associating with people you would not normally associate with or would usually actively avoid dealing with; and (4) reading magazines and books you would not normally read. While it is well-known that hiring people with diverse academic, cultural, and physical capabilities and backgrounds brings diversity to a team, we must remember that we can also promote creativity by taking the uncomfortable step of deliberately cultivating "the fringe" by finding people who we know disagree with our current decision and reap that diversity of opinion (Godin, 2005). We will discuss this in more detail later in this chapter.

DeBono (1969), one of the most well-known creativity proponents, discussed the importance of random, unplanned stimulation via brainstorming, cross-disciplinary discussion, deliberate exposure to irrelevant stimuli, or random word stimulation (e.g., opening a dictionary and pointing to a random word on a random page and trying to associate the word with the issue or problem at hand).

I think it has a lot do with how you expose yourself to other things, like if you go into a showroom or you see something that really inspires you in some nicely designed shops. If I lived in a concrete box my whole life and never saw anything else,

I don't think I'd be thinking of all these fantastic ideas. (Julia, Architect)

Different countries and people bring concepts native to their culture or industry and introduce them in a new context that is seen as creative. (Richard, Graphic and Digital Multimedia Designer)

Random stimulation can also come from the application of any one of a number of well-known surrealist techniques (Kneeshaw, 2005, 2006). "Surrealism is an artistic, cultural and intellectual movement oriented toward the liberation of the mind by emphasizing the critical and imaginative faculties of the 'unconscious mind' and the attainment of a dream-like state different from, 'more than,' and ultimately 'truer' than everyday reality: the 'sur-real,' or 'more than real'" (http://en.wikipedia.org/wiki/Surrealist). Designers build upon the results of their research with a mixture of creativity and commercial insight and often find that ideas that may seem strange at first are often worth exploring and that the "common-sense" solution is not always the right one (Design Council UK, 2006). Designers often generate counterintuitive concepts that turn out to be winners in the end because they are unconventional. This is the definition of a strategy innovation, and surrealist techniques can help us get there by providing structured methods for random stimulation that enable us to think things we have never thought before.

Surrealist techniques can be language-based, visual or intellectual (e.g., interpretation and alteration), and individual- or group-based (cf. Brotchie, 1995). For example, a classic surrealist-inspired technique used to help writers unblock their thinking is to ask each member of a group to write a definite or indefinite article (e.g., the, a, an) and an adjective (e.g., hot, tall, red, excited) on a piece of paper, then fold the paper over what is written and pass it to someone else. The next person writes a noun (e.g., house, dog, car) and folds the paper over that. The third person writes down a verb (e.g., run, sleep, throw) and the process is repeated. When the randomly generated words are revealed, some small grammatical changes may be necessary, but you will have a rudimentary sentence such as these taken from Brotchie's excellent *A Book of Surrealist Games* (1995): "The exquisite corpse shall drink new wine" or "The avenged topaz shall devour with kisses the paralytic of Rome" (p. 25). While these sentences make no sense, because of the random combinations of words, that is precisely their value. They can be used to provide stimulation and spark new directions in our thinking when applied to particular problems, products/services, experiences, business models, or industries.

Identify and Violate Assumptions

A fourth technique for stimulating creativity is to identify and then violate or continuously question our assumptions. As mentioned in chapter two in relation to the brief, this is a technique particularly well-used by designers. This is especially important for strategy innovation as it is often our preconceived assumptions and what has been done in the past that stop us from trying new things. While this questioning of assumptions also sounds easy in theory, it is difficult to do in reality. It requires recognizing that what we think we know to be true is actually something we assume to be true. In a sense, it requires unlearning what we know.

In terms of research and ideation I first use free association and do a great deal of sketching. I do lots until I get stuck. Second, I find existing examples. Third, I try and develop a set of rules or a grammar for the design process so that I can break those rules deliberately later on. I identify the assumptions and then deliberately break them. (Ron, Graphic Design)

Make explicit assumptions and challenge them later. (Frank, Graphic Designer)

Mukherji and Mukherji (2003) applied this thinking to strategy and discussed it in terms of the concept of "deframing." They stated, "popular frames in strategy should be subject to deframing. Deframing is important because people generally do not know how to abandon the ways of thinking and acting that they have learned to rely on and are not even aware that it is an issue" (pp. 4–5). I had some clients from the telecommunications industry look at their current strategy statements and identify all of the assumptions they could find associated with them. Many basic assumptions such as "we are and will always be a telecommunications company," "everyone will have a mobile phone in the future," "our major competitors are and will continue to be company X and company Y," "people will continue to be willing to purchase pre-paid phone cards" were identified. We then deliberately violated and questioned each assumption and used the new perspectives we gained to generate some creative thoughts about innovative strategic opportunities for the future.

It's asking the question a different way. How can we get people to think that this is actually a good thing instead of assuming it's a bad thing? I worked with a Ski Village, some years ago. They decided that they were going to buy these huge machines to produce snow...the problem was that when they turned them on at night the sound was so loud people were not going to be able to sleep and they would complain about it. So they had all these meetings about how can we insulate this thing so it doesn't sound so loud and they were talking, talking, talking about it and no one could come up with a solution that was economically viable. It was either isolate the bloody thing, which had a lot of technical problems, or double glaze all the windows in the village and all those sorts of things which will cost a fortune. So, they were in this meeting and a marketing guy showed up and said, "Hold on. You're making snow and this is why people come here. That's fantastic. Let's say we're making the snow for tomorrow. You'll have the best snow tomorrow morning and people will understand and not mind the noise so much." It was a beautiful solution. We will sell a bad thing and say we're making the snow for you for tomorrow. Who would complain? You know you will go to sleep thinking about tomorrow's skiing...it will be perfect snow, soft and white, sweet dreams. (Eberto, Architect)

Similar to the concept of deframing mentioned earlier, is the concept of defamiliarization. Light, Blythe, and Reed (2007) suggested defamiliarization techniques can be used to help us think creatively and imagine things differently. The concept of defamiliarization is critical to good design and strategy innovation because when things become familiar and commonplace, we fail to think creatively about them. By defamiliarizing them, we place them in a new context, juxtapose them with something novel, and we can see them in a new light. The process highlights our most basic taken-for-granted assumptions about things, and allows us to challenge and violate them once identified leading to novel and creative solutions and ideas.

For example, metonymic substitution is a defamiliarization technique that draws attention to meaning by questioning the dominant description of something (Light, Blythe, and Reed, 2007). It uses inversion for its defamiliarization effect. In other words, we replace a common descriptor with its opposite. A portable device (e.g., computer, cell-phone, MP3 player, PDA) becomes a luggable or a losable device highlighting that laptops were quite heavy at first and needed to be lighter and that cell phones may be portable but they are also losable leading to the design of ways they can become attachable or findable. Another method Light, Blythe, and Reed (2007, p. 68) discussed is random scenario-building (a combination of random qualities in a scenario-building process that opens up the social aspects of the situation as a prelude to considering intervention). Novel combinations of pairings of a role (nouns such as mother, teenager, business-person) and role descriptors (adjectives such as aged, drug-pushing, limping) confound social expectations, highlight assumptions and stereotypes (e.g., drug-pushing mother, aged teenager, limping business-person), and can lead to novel ideas and creative solutions.

Expression and Emotional Release

Another technique for creatively generating novel concepts and ideas is emotional expression and release. Deborah Kneeshaw, a graphic artist and design educator, and I together ran several executive programs on creative strategic thinking in 1995/1996 with managers and executives from a number of organizations. Deborah would ask participants to use color to draw, sketch, and paint, while at the same time move around and listen to music. Participants were instructed to relax, and express themselves and their emotions during the exercises. Many people found these seemingly simple activities profoundly meaningful and emotionally moving. Once given permission, the appropriate tools, a context of relevance and importance, and an appropriate physical work environment, they were able to express and release emotions surprisingly well. In another exercise, participants would cut out images from magazines and create mood-boards that were collages of related images expressing certain qualities or attributes of a person or group (similar to the character profiles we discussed in chapter three). These methods of expression were quite foreign to the majority of the managers and executives who participated in the programs. The exercises required participants to think symbolically and to express themselves creatively. The point for us here is that I continually noticed that with emotional expression and release creativity came inevitably.

Incubation

Finally, we come to the other side of the story about creativity. While we know a great deal about many techniques to help us be creative, there is also an undeniable element of intuition, insight, and blinding flashes of inspiration sometimes involved in the process. The importance of incubation—taking breaks from the problem—for successful problem-solving, creativity, and design is well established (Bundy, 2002; Cross, 2000; Pilditch, 1990; Sowrey, 1987). According to Russo (2006) it has been suggested that

> In creativity research, we refer to the three Bs—for the bathtub, the bed and the bus—places where ideas have famously and suddenly emerged. When we take time off from working on a problem, we change what we're doing and our context, and that can activate different areas of our brain. If the answer wasn't in the part of the brain we were using, it might be in another. If we're lucky, in the next context we may hear or see something that relates—distantly—to the problem that we had temporarily put aside ... even when an idea seems sudden, our minds have actually been working on it all along. (pp. 89–90)

> I do a lot of work in my mind while doing other things than designing. (Anne, Product Designer)

> With creativity you also sometimes just walk away and revisit it later. (Kay, Interior Designer)

> The inspiration can come to you while you are peeling potatoes. (Lynda, Graphic Designer, Book Designer)

Cross (2000) suggested that taking a holiday, talking the problem over with colleagues and friends, tackling another problem, and enlarging the search space are all good incubation techniques to promote design creativity. Another way to allow time for ideas to incubate is to work on several projects at the same time. This way when you need to take a break from one project for a while, you can work on something else and still be productive. Of course, engaging in restful, relaxing diversions also allows time for incubation. According to Osborn (1953), "the term [incubation] covers the phenomenon by which ideas spontaneously well up into our consciousness. Incubation often results in 'bright' ideas, and perhaps that's why it is said to invite illumination" (p. 160). Sleep, relaxation, working on something else, and allowing lots of time for creative projects are all ways that can help incubation to stimulate creativity.

Creativity and Strategy Innovation: A Diversity of Inputs

The design literature suggests broad participation in the design process leads to more creativity, and a better understanding of and solution to the problem. Involvement of diverse stakeholders provides a wide range of expertise, increases the amount and variety of information available, and leads to a better understanding of critical problems (Brown and Eisenhardt, 1995; Bundy, 2002; Clegg, 1999; Godin, 2005). It has been suggested that we need diversity to be creative and that we should bring in outsiders and novices who know little or nothing about our problems and, therefore, have no preconceived notions or assumptions about what can and cannot be done. It is no surprise, Kim (1990) stated, "that major innovations in a field often originate from sources external to it. Outsiders are often unaware of limitations that may have hampered traditional work in a given field, but which no longer hold. Moreover, newcomers bring to bear a fresh panorama of attitudes, skills, and know-how" (p. 12). The basic advice from designers and the design literature, therefore, is to involve and get agreement from as many stakeholders as possible.

> Use teams to review your options and get ideas. You can get trapped into one way of thinking and the team can give you ideas. (Catroina, Architect)

> I give an idea to someone I know who does not like the idea. This way we test it quite differently from those who design it. (Brad, Museum Design Manager)

> …and always get feedback from another. Having other designers around you and getting feedback is critical. (Kay, Interior Designer)

> We review designs at various stages "on the wall" just as you do at architecture school. Where possible, we involve everyone in the office in these (we are seven in total). This allows the intelligence and experience in the office to be disseminated across projects. (Christopher, Architect)

> Creativity is about working with others, the peer thing is how it works. I give the students an idea, they go outside and sit around the table and make it work. It's the student community that makes it work. (Robert, Product Designer, Design Educator)

> The "secret sauce" is the collaboration of the research team. We mix engineers with designers, service people, and people from manufacturing and sales. There is no question about it, software design and development is better with ongoing collaboration. (Philip, Industrial Designer)

As mentioned in chapter two in relation to the brief, several authors have also discussed the importance of diversity of input to the strategy development process (cf. Carr and Pearson, 2002; Farnham and Horton, 2003; Liedtka and Rosenblum, 1996; Wall and Wall, 1995). Hamel (1997) suggested that new voices must be heard as part of the strategy development process; not just the voices of senior managers and strategists:

> New genetic material must be brought into the strategy process. Diversity was a requirement for the development of life; so too is it a requirement for the emergence of new strategy... Strategy depends not only on a diversity of voices but on the connections between those voices... we need new conversations—conversations that cross the boundaries of function, technology, hierarchy, business, and geography. One thing is certain: If for five or six years in a row the same ten or fifteen people in a company have the same conversations about strategy in the same way, new insights will be unlikely to emerge. Strategizing depends on creating a rich and complex web of conversations that cut across previously isolated pockets of knowledge and create new and unexpected combinations of insight... Great strategy requires new ways of seeing. Redefining what a company does best constitutes a new way of seeing. Also, looking at your products or services differently can help... Opportunities for innovative strategy don't emerge from sterile analysis and number crunching—they emerge from novel experiences that can create opportunities for novel insights. (pp. 75–76)

In other words, when you need to decide among already defined choices, or you have to solve a well-defined problem, or if the future is a linear extrapolation of the past, the best approach is often a rational decision-making process (March and Simon 1958; Riley, 1998; Surowiecki, 2004). However, this is not always the case with more complex design and strategy innovation problems where alternatives are not known or knowable, or when decision criteria are not available or are conflicting or ambiguous, or when the future must be created as it is not there to be discovered by analysis. The need for user involvement and participation in the process of the creative definition and solution of complex "wicked" problems has been illustrated convincingly (Blythe, Grabill, and Riley, 2008; Conklin, 2006; Durant and Legge, 2006; Kreuter et al., 2004; Rittel and Webber, 1973).

It is the same with strategy innovation. It is a complicated process. Not all alternatives are known or knowable. Decision criteria are often not available or are conflicting or ambiguous. The future must be actively created, not discovered already existing via analysis. The smart thing to do in this case is to involve a variety of stakeholders to participate. Remember, quantity of ideas wins over quality at first. This is where creativity and discovery come in. Once many possible alternatives are uncovered, we can then add in more rational and technical methods when trying to decide among them.

Therefore, the two keys to using participation to successfully create strategy innovations are the decentralization of information gathering involving a large number of people to promote diversity of inputs and creativity, and using these diverse inputs and appropriate creativity techniques to generate a large range of strategic alternatives and possibilities. If, for example, you need to "predict" the future, in the sense of generating strategy innovations and making a strategic "prediction," a good way to do it would be to use your "internal market." Gather together a number of small groups (about fifteen–twenty people in each group), invite a small number of analysts and outside experts to add their opinions, and get them all to think as creatively as possible (e.g., using appropriate techniques from those outlined earlier) and to generate as many options as they can. Remember, designers are telling us that success comes from an early focus on a diversity of inputs leading to a large quantity of ideas, not an early focus on the expert and on finding the one "right" answer.

Relying on the strategy experts is a flawed tactic according to some. For example, Surowiecki (2004) suggested the following:

> There is no real evidence that one can become expert in something as broad as "decision-making" or "policy" or "strategy." Auto repair, piloting, skiing, perhaps even management: these are skills that yield to application, hard work, and native talent. But forecasting an uncertain future and deciding the best course of action in the face of that future are much less likely to do so. And much of what we've seen so far suggests that a large group of diverse individuals will come up with a better and more robust forecast and make more intelligent decisions than even the most skilled "decision-maker." (p. 32)

While this flies in the face of much of what happens in many businesses and what is taught in many business schools around the globe,

Surowiecki (2004) is not alone in his suggestion. Mukherji and Mukherji (2003) also suggested

> it is extraordinarily difficult, perhaps impossible, to train strategists. Success in strategy calls for a quality of judgement that cannot be taught. There is scope for individual ability or aptitude at the tactical and operational levels where sound training for consistently superior performance can be provided. Strategic excellence cannot be taught the same way. (p. 6)

This perspective suggests that strategy innovation is inherently a group, rather than an individual, process. The concept of crowd-sourcing is relevant here. Crowd-sourcing is outsourcing something to many people. Joyce (2008) has shown that crowd-sourcing can be used to encourage creativity, and to produce a large quantity of original, diverse quality solutions to problems. I am suggesting we can benefit by crowd-sourcing the creation of strategy innovations.

At this point in the creative concept generation process, the keys to success are: (1) the use of both hard work and incubation; (2) generating many ideas and solutions as quantity over quality at first is critical; (3) using many techniques for generating solutions, concepts, and ideas such as creative combination and alteration, the appropriate physical work environment, random stimulation, identifying and violating assumptions, incubation, the expression and release of emotions, and a diversity of inputs; and (4) we need to involve many people, both from inside and outside of our organizations, in the creative strategy generation process. The traditional distinction between strategy formulation or development, done by a small group of senior managers and experts, and strategy implementation or execution, which is carried out by the rest of the employees based on the senior management blueprint, is fundamentally flawed and, as we have seen, is not likely to generate successful strategy innovation.

CHAPTER FIVE

Prototyping: Making an Idea Clearly Visible

The distinguishing element within the development and evaluation phase of the design process is the prototype (Archer, 1979; Baskerville and Stage, 1996; Cross, 1982; Rainey, 2005; Ulrich and Eppinger, 2004). Prototypes are essential for good design as they help designers learn if something will work and how well it meets the specified needs. Prototypes can be used to help communicate a concept as "a picture is worth a thousand words." They help make the unknown visible and the unfamiliar real. Prototypes can also be used to ensure that components and subsystems work together as expected. Mature prototypes can be used to demonstrate functionality and as progress milestones. Finally, a prototype gives us something to try and, at the same time, not break the bank.

> Prototyping and visualisation are the defining characteristics of the design process. You can either say, "What is the smartest way I can work out the right answer?" or you can completely flip the problem and say, "Is there a way I can make it affordable to change my mind?" That is what a prototype gives us. (Andrew, Designer, Management Consultant)

> Prototyping is critical. (Robert, Product Designer, Design Educator)

> The design process is always going back and forth. What you see in the beginning is not what happens in the end. What you envisage in the beginning could end up not being what it's going to be in the end because once you start it, other people get involved. Obviously the client's involved again...you have other feedback which keeps coming in and out all the time so that [it] develops. (Connie, Architect)

My biggest challenge [as a design educator] is helping people change their two-dimensional thinking into three-dimensional thinking. (Rod, Illustrator and Design Educator)

I design with pencil and paper, and I build physical connections between what I think and do. The connection between the creative thought and the physical outcome is it. (John, Media Designer)

A picture may be worth one thousand words, but a flash proto-type is worth one million. (Philip, Industrial Designer)

Unfortunately prototyping is not often considered as part of the strat-egy development process. While various strategic scenarios are some-times considered (cf. Drew, 2006; van der Heijden, 2005), the idea that it is important to experiment, make the abstract real, try many things, get feedback, and play around with various ideas and strategic models to see how well they work is not part of the typical strategy develop-ment process. There is a good deal strategy innovators can learn about prototyping from designers. In the remainder of this chapter, therefore, we will explore how designers use prototypes and how prototyping can be used to help create strategy innovations.

Prototyping and Design: Nothing was Ever Invented and Perfected at the Same Time

Cross (1982, p. 221) and Archer (1979, p. 20) in two of the seminal papers aimed at establishing the theoretical bases for treating design as a coherent discipline of study, defined design as the collected experience of the material culture, and the collected body of experience, skills, and understanding embodied in the arts of planning, inventing, making, and doing, which has at its core the language of modeling. This lan-guage of modeling is a language of the visual or physical representation of ideas. In other words, design has at its very core, the process of pro-totyping; that is, quickly making up a visual or physical representation or model so we can see it, touch it, play with it, and try it out.

Kimbell et al. (1990) discussed several ways of modeling solutions that range from simple discussion (i.e., informal modeling), which is quick and easy and helps us get a grip on some of the issues that might need to be addressed, through to diagrammatic or computer simulated modeling, which enables finer details to be explored and resolved, to graphic techniques and 3-D models that fully represent the look and feel of a finished idea or product. Strategy scenarios are slightly more complicated versions of the simple discussion and probably fit somewhere between there and the diagrammatic or computer simulated model if we were to think of Kimbell's types as a continuum.

Regardless of the form a prototype takes, however, they are seen as critical elements in the design process (Archer, 1979; Baskerville and Stage, 1996; Cross, 1982; Dodgson, Gann, and Salter, 2005; Gierke, Hanson, and Turner, 2002; Godin, 2005; Nadler, 1980). Russo (2006) provided a good historically familiar example of the value of prototypes:

> Take the first aeroplane. On December 8, 1903 Samuel Pierpont Langley, a leading government-funded scientist, launched with much fanfare his flying machine on the Potomac. It plummeted into the river. Nine days later, Orville and Wilbur Wright got the first plane off the ground. Why did these bicycle mechanics succeed when a famous scientist failed? Because Langley hired other people to execute his concept. Studying the Wright's diaries, you see that insight and execution are inextricably woven together. Over years, as they solved problems like wing shape and wing warping, each adjustment involved a small spark of insight that led to others. (p. 90)

In other words, we see that successful designers use prototypes to refine their initial ideas before locking in on one solution.

> Prototyping is important because you have to create something that has to be tested physically; it has to materialize into reality. You must be able to imagine it to do that. (Kay, Interior Designer)

> We always build significant prototypes. The key is to get it in front of customers early and often for feedback. (Philip, Industrial Designer)

An example of this is how I devised the structure I have used to write some of the chapters and subsections of this book. The structure is roughly: (1) introduction to the topic; (2) some quotes from the designers interviewed; (3) discussion of the relevant design literature; and (4) comparison to the traditional strategy development process. This structure was something I discovered over time, after many rounds of trial and error, experimentation, and prototyping. I did not have it in mind at the start and then execute it. It almost seems like it magically emerged, but it was a result of effort and learning from many iterations of prototypes and feedback, and much trial and error.

According to Schrage (2000), the MIT Media Lab's unofficial credo is "Demo or Die!" and it even appears on the face of a fourth floor clock in lieu of numbers. This captures the prevailing belief at the MIT Media Lab that it is not enough to have brilliant ideas; you have to be able to demonstrate them. The way to successfully innovate, according to Schrage (2000), is through prototyping (models, simulations, etc.) and then "show and ask" rather than "show and tell." How many of us when trying to develop strategy are willing and able to "play" with our ideas? How many of us think about strategy development as an exciting, creative opportunity to innovate, play, show, ask, and learn?

Rapid Prototyping

Another lesson strategy developers can learn from designers is about the importance of rapid, "quick and dirty" prototypes. As with good design, during the early stages of strategy innovation development, perfection should not be the goal. We should not be looking for the one right answer. We should at first simply generate and explore various ideas and possibilities.

> I do research, and work and rework and put the output into visual techniques like sketches, charts and graphs, and take it to 3-D or a model or something sculptural to look at form. I visualize ideas in my head at the start and get them on paper to test them and see if they work as a form or space. (Todd, Interior Designer, Design Educator)

The goal with rapid prototypes is to develop and explore options that take us in the right direction quickly and inexpensively, and progressively refine them through repeated experimentation and iterative adjustment. Consider the examples (see figure 5.1) provided by Todd Packer.[1] In this series of sketches we can see how he started with some quick rough sketches (panels 1 and 2) exploring two shapes he had in mind. He then took those shapes and played with them in different ways exploring their relationships to each other, to people, and to other interior elements (panels 3–6). In sketch 7 he puts it together so it looks more like an office. In sketch 8 he goes backward (iterates)

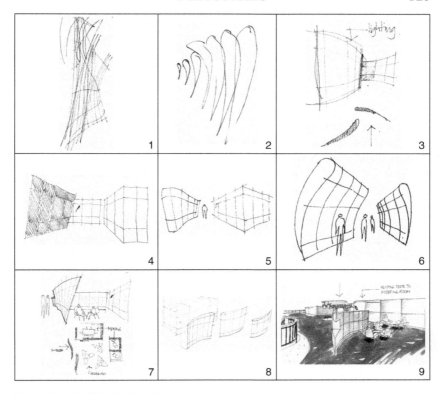

Figure 5.1 Todd Packer interior concepts.

to explore the relationships between form and space. Finally, in sketch 9 we see something that has progressed to a more mature and recognizable representation.

Rapid prototyping has been shown to successfully help evaluate functionality, and to save time and money in the new product development process (Dutson and Wood, 2005; Evans and Campbell, 2003). In order to be useful, however, prototypes do not need to be elaborate or expensive. In fact, quite the contrary is true.

Prototypes should command only as much time, effort, and investment as are needed to generate useful feedback and evolve an idea. The more "finished" a prototype seems, the less likely its creators will be to pay attention to and profit from feedback. The goal of prototyping isn't to finish. It is to learn about the strengths and weaknesses of the idea and to identify new directions that further prototypes might take. (Brown, 2008, p. 87)

We physically make crappy models just so we can see it. (Robert, Product Designer, Design Educator)

The value of a rapid prototype is that it helps people experience a possible future in tangible ways. Quick-and-dirty models and prototypes give us license to experiment and explore hunches or directions that may lead to radical strategy innovations or, at least, give more clarity to the problem statement.

The best thing that we, as designers, can add is that we can create a richly rendered and articulated view of what the future can be; a rich representation of what is possible that comes from a deliberate process. (Philip, Industrial Designer)

An example of how rapid prototyping can help us make strategic-level decisions in organizations comes from Eason (1997) who discussed the case where a freight forwarding company was implementing a major computer system. The company had two different scenarios in mind for the application of the system (one involved centralization and the other decentralization of information). The company piloted the system in one region and tried both the centralized and decentralized information options. The centralized "consolidation" approach met some important business objectives but proved to have some serious negative implications for branch manager autonomy. "At the end of the trial the company decided that they had to preserve this entrepreneurial spirit which was the basis of the energy of the company and they abandoned load consolidation in favour of independent branches" (p. 6).

Consider the following example (see figure 5.2) from Karen Lewis[2] and her students at the College of Design at the University of Kentucky. They were using various architectural principles to explore the potential redesign of the Bluegrass Stockyard in Lexington, Kentucky. In this example, you can see that they prototyped several options (exploring various percentages of space dedicated to parking, landscape, and manure) and graphically represented them, followed by a rendition of what the final outcome might look like. This helped all stakeholders to visualize what the outcome might be, and helped them visualize and explore various options, and combinations of options.

MANU(RE)MANAGEMENT
How manure, parking and landscape might configure
to protect, augment, and support each other

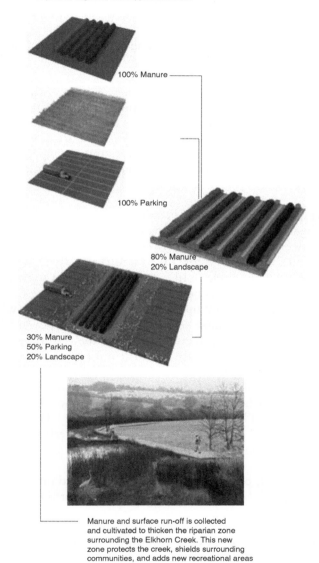

100% Manure

100% Parking

80% Manure
20% Landscape

30% Manure
50% Parking
20% Landscape

Manure and surface run-off is collected
and cultivated to thicken the riparian zone
surrounding the Elkhorn Creek. This new
zone protects the creek, shields surrounding
communities, and adds new recreational areas

Figure 5.2 Manure management.

The results of all of this playing, modeling and tinkering are cheaper mistakes and faster solutions. Successful companies see the value in making as many mistakes as possible early in the design process when they can learn the most at the lowest risk and cost (Lajocono and Zaccai, 2004).

> Fail early, fail often, prototype, test, and move on. (Alex, Industrial Designer)

We must be able to do the same thing when designing strategy innovations. We must not wait until something is perfected before implementing it. We must learn from designers how to be iterative, which is the opposite of waiting until something is right before doing anything. We must learn by doing, by trial and error, and by experimentation. This naturally involves prototyping, honing, and refining through multiple iterations.

> Prototyping is great at forcing people to confront biases that they haven't been able to articulate to date. We used this for KPI [key performance indicator] reports. We could have done an econometric analysis of the business for three months and then worked out what the reports should look like. But because I was a green consultant, and just two years before that I was a practising designer, I went ahead and mocked up a report without really knowing if any of the staff could make sense of it. What was powerful was we were able to start argument on some of the cognitive aspects of the outcome. There is only so much information the human mind can comprehend. So the minute you throw a mocked-up report in front of somebody you can start to get useful feedback like "I can get my head around that" or "I don't know how to read those charts" or "There are too many numbers" or "There are not enough numbers," or whatever. That is very powerful. (Andrew, Designer, Management Consultant)

Nussbaum (2004, p. 5) discussed some of the rapid prototyping tips and techniques used by the innovative design team at IDEO:

- *Mock up everything.* It is possible to create models not only of products but also of services such as health care, air-travel, and spaces such as museum lobbies, waiting areas/rooms, and offices. As we mentioned in chapter three when we discussed research under the topic of "trying," there is great value in becoming your customer.

A prototype or mock journey that describes, outlines, or enacts a typical customer experience can provide valuable insights for strategy innovation.

- *Go fast. No frills.* Build prototypes and models quickly and cheaply. Never waste time on complicated concepts. Remember, we are not concerned at this point in the design process with getting it right. We are concerned with initial development, generating and exploring ideas, and with learning from feedback and experience. We are making prototypes that demonstrate a design idea without sweating over the details.

We can see that designers seem to use rapidly developed working models and prototypes to gain feedback, to help everyone involved visualize possible solutions, and to speed up decision-making, learning, and innovation. These are the very things we want to do as designers of strategy innovations.

Involving Stakeholders in Development via Prototyping

The third thing strategy developers can learn from designers related to prototyping is about the importance of involving customers in the development process by exposing them to prototypes. As Schrage (2000) suggested, if we talk to users and come up with a user specification, as is often done with software development, and then go away and perfect the answer, when we come back and show it to the client they will, more often than not, respond with something like, "Well, you have given us almost exactly what we discussed. The problem is, now that we actually see it, we realize that is not at all what we really want. What we really want you to do is..." (p. 18). Alternatively, what we should be doing is making the client a partner in the development process and doing a series of rapid, "quick and dirty" prototypes of various strategic models or options continually seeking feedback, and exploring and refining ideas, until we run out of time or money, or we hone in on the problem and its solution.

The more you involve the client at the beginning, the more responsibility they take for the outcome. (Simon, Illustrator, Graphic Designer)

It is clear that user involvement in prototyping is important for successful innovation. Rather than work on one design, fall in love with it, and jam it down the throats of users, the great designer engages users in a collaborative process of testing and refining to help the design rapidly evolve to the point where it delights users. Involving users in prototyping can lead to a solution the designer couldn't have otherwise contemplated. (Martin, 2005b). One-sided relationships between the company and its clients (users react, they do not propose) are being superseded by "envisioning laboratories," environments in which users can play with new technologies before an application has been packaged as a finished product. Pre-prototyping user needs has obvious benefits (Thackara, 1997).

Prototyping Reduces Risk

One of the obvious benefits of prototyping, and a fourth lesson strategy developers can learn from designers, is that prototyping helps reduce risk. For example, designers have been using prototyping to reduce risk in information systems and software development for many years (Baskerville and Stage, 1996; Pressman, 1982; Schrage, 2000). An example of this comes from a case written by Reynolds and Yetton (2006), wherein they described how before the Commonwealth Bank in Australia went live with their new Commonwealth Securities (CommSec) business, offering online trading to the public, they experimented on bank staff. According to the bank's operations manager at the time, on day one, when they had no client base, they decided to experiment with Commonwealth Bank staff and invite them to open accounts and trade using the new systems before they went out to the public and offered a service that they may, or may not, have been able to fully deliver at the time. This type of prototyping helped them try out systems, technology, processes, and procedures, and get them right before going live.

Applied to strategy innovation, while in the short run it may look like we are increasing the number of times we are failing, as long as we learn from our trials, and we keep them relatively quick and inexpensive, we will always be moving forward and in the longer-term we will derive great benefits.

So from the leadership perspective we can say, "I'm confident I need to head down this path," but the question we need to answer is "Exactly what will that look like?" While with the design process we can show people what it will look like, we cannot argue that we have exhausted all the other options. This exhausting possibilities is at the heart of the risk management approach where we cutaway degrees of freedom in business. Design does not do that. The two processes, therefore, are very different. (Andrew, Designer, Management Consultant)

While it is true that we cannot exhaust all possible options, prototyping is a risk mitigation tactic as we, at the very least, know whether or not what we have tried works. When we involve customers in the proto- typing process, we learn what many people think about the idea, and we receive and can incorporate feedback through multiple iterations. We have known for years that pilot-testing and prototyping increase the success of technology implementation and organizational change (cf. Rogers, 1995; Tornatzky and Klein, 1982; Zaltman, Duncan, and Holbek, 1973). Designers show us that pilot-testing and prototyping will also increase the likelihood of successful design and implementa- tion of the strategy innovations we develop.

How Prototyping can Help Develop Strategy Innovations

There are two main ways that prototyping can help us to generate strategy innovations. The first is by giving us a structured method for experimentation and learning leading to successful strategy innovation. The second is by helping to make strategy visible so we can gain feed- back and insight into the effects of strategic options.

Experimentation and Innovation: Emergent Strategy Innovation by Design

Prototypes, pilot-tests, models, and simulations can help us create strat- egy innovations by generating surprises and by challenging, rather than confirming, our initial ideas and assumptions. According to Schrage (2000), "The real value of a model or simulation may stem less from its ability to test a hypothesis than from its power to generate useful surprize" (p. 117). Models and prototypes will serve our strategy inno- vation efforts best when they surprise us, and challenge our ideas and assumptions, leading to something new.

I'm working on an illustration for a game company right now that has evolved considerably since my first briefing on the scope of the project because I keep adding elements to it, which the client is surprised by, causing them to have me take it even further. (Troy, Graphic Designer and Illustrator)

Some of the things designers do well are to produce novel unexpected solutions and concepts; second is the ability to tolerate uncertainty and to work with incomplete information; the third is the use of imagination and constructive forethought; and the fourth is the use of drawings and other modelling media as means of problem solving. (Geoff, Design Educator)

The difference between design and engineering is surprise. For example, we are trying to bring software to this hardware company. We learned by happy accident, along with a great deal of customer research, that we can use our products as robust data gathering devices. Some designers and researchers exploring various options said "What happens if we try this?" It has turned out to be a great idea. (Philip, Industrial Designer)

This is the core of the innovation process that helps us to generate something new. Unfortunately, research indicates that when thinking and making decisions, people are frequently overconfident, risk averse, only seek confirming evidence, and assume the feedback received is both complete and reliable (Kahneman and Tversky, 1979a and b; Lovallo and Kahneman, 2003; Schoemaker and Gunther, 2006). Because of this, we tend to be afraid of making mistakes, and we do not learn as well or as quickly as we could.

When fundamental assumptions are wrong, companies can achieve success more quickly by deliberately making errors than by considering only data that supports the assumptions. Research shows that executives who apply a conventional, systematic approach to solving a pattern recognition problem are often slower to find a solution than those who test their assumptions by knowingly making mistakes. (Schoemaker and Gunther, 2006, p. 104)

Awareness of our biases and preconceived notions, and of our habits and mindsets born of years of education, training, and experience, is critical for success as our biases, habits, and mindsets can blind us to new possibilities, perspectives, and viewpoints (cf. Lovallo and Kahneman, 2003). By using pilot-tests, prototypes, models, or simulations, strategy innovators act as creative experimenters, continually testing ideas and learning through a deliberate process of enlightened trial and error (Kelley, 2005).

Emergent strategy has been contrasted with more deliberate strategic planning and development processes for many years (cf. Bruce,

Lampel, and Mintzberg, 1999; Mintzberg and Waters, 1985). More recently, emergent strategy has been associated with the notions of strategy as simple rules (cf. Bonabeau and Meyer, 2001; Eisenhardt and Sull, 2001; Gadiesh and Gilbert, 2001) and with the idea that strategy is sometimes a process of focused trial and error or experimentation (cf. Hodgkinson, 2002; Liedtka and Rosenblum, 1996; Pitt and Clarke, 1999). An example of this, and of how the results of experimentation and trials can surprise us, challenge our ideas and assumptions, and help us develop strategy innovations, comes from some work I did with a global telecommunications company. In one of their call centers, they were looking for ways to help telephone customer service representatives provide an excellent customer experience. We ended up trialing the simple rule to "give a customer credit whenever you, the person on the telephone with the customer, think it is deserved." Our idea was that this would empower staff, encourage them to take personal responsibility for their decisions based on their interactions with the customer, reduce the need for policies, procedures, and for supervisory involvement, and lead to quicker more reasonable decisions and, therefore, to an excellent customer experience. In the first month, people were taking significant personal responsibility and making decisions without involving supervisors. This was good and expected, or at least hoped-for. What was so surprising was that following this simple rule also led to a 50 percent reduction in the dollar-value of customer credit given. We did not expect this at all. What was even more unexpected was a further 50 percent reduction in the dollar-value of customer credit given in the second month. There was no way to predict this a priori. The experiment led to a surprising result, and illustrated the power and complexity of this innovation related to customer service interactions.

Hamel (1997) realized the importance of experimentation in strategy development and of making our strategies and their effects visible:

Passion and foresight will only get you so far. When it comes to executing a strategy, the end target may be clearly visible—"I want to climb that mountain over there"—but much of the route may be invisible from the starting point. The only way you're going to see the path ahead is to start moving. Thus strategy is as much about experimentation as it is about foresight and passion.

In many organizations, the quest for efficiency drives out experimentation. One question I often ask managers: "Can you point to 20 or 30 small experiments going on in your company that you believe could fundamentally remake your company?" In most cases, the answer is no, there is nothing to point to.

In the new economy, we are attempting to explore vast spaces of possibility—how genetics will remake medicine, how biotech will change the chemical industry, how interactive technology will change the very idea of a university, and so on. (p. x)

In this case where the future is unclear, and may be even unknowable until we get there, the only possible way forward is via experimentation and trial and error. As with all wickedly complex problems, the strategy innovation creation process is characterized by the following [adapted from Cross (2000), who was discussing design problems, and Conklin (2006), and Rittel and Webber (1973), who were discussing complex, wicked policy and social problems]:

1. There is no definitive formulation of the problem. You cannot understand the problem until you have developed and trialed a solution or two. Every solution tried exposes new aspects of the problem, requiring further adjustments to the potential solutions. Proposing and experimenting with solutions is the only means of understanding the problem. Many assumptions about the problem, and specific areas of uncertainty, can be exposed only by proposing and trialing solutions. Many constraints and criteria emerge as a result of evaluating solutions. In other words, trial and error are inevitable.
2. Goals are usually vague, and many constraints and criteria (e.g., stopping rules) are unknown. Any problem formulation may embody inconsistencies. Many conflicts and inconsistencies have to be resolved in the solution. Once again, trial and error are inevitable for this to happen.
3. Wicked problems have no given alternative solutions. There may be no solutions, or there may be a host of potential solutions that are devised, and many others that are never even thought of. It is a matter of creativity to devise potential solutions, and a matter of trial and error to determine which are valid, and which should be pursued and implemented.

That is why strategy innovation must be a process of deliberate focused trial and error. The only way of understanding a complex, wicked strategy problem and of creating solutions to it is by conducting experiments, launching pilot programs, testing prototypes, and being surprised by, and continually learning from, the results.

According to Hamel (1997), if we ask the question, "How will the Internet remake industry structures?" it does not matter how many gurus, consultants, and dollars we throw at it, the answer is still going to be at least partly unclear (p. 16). The breadth of experimentation must be related to the degree of unknowability that confronts the asker. The more we experiment, the faster we can learn which strategies are more likely to work. As we learned with prototyping, the goal here is not to develop perfect strategies. The goal is to develop strategies quickly (i.e., rapid prototyping) that take us in the right direction and progressively refine them through repeated experimentation and iterative adjustment. If our goal is to generate strategy innovation, new and radical business models, new ways of delivering unprecedented value, the development of whole new industries, and the solution to some of our most intractable social and financial problems, we must experiment in uncharted territory so we can create and explore novel solutions. The answers are not out there for our analyses to discover. It is through focused trial and error, and through iterative pilot-testing and prototyping that we will achieve this, not through a single, blindingly brilliant insight that reveals the one true right answer.

Making Strategy Visible: Computer Modeling Strategy

The second way prototyping can help us generate strategy innovations is by making the effects of strategy visible so we can gain feedback and insight into the effects of various options. According to Plach, Wallach, and Wintermantel (1999), "Empirical investigations have demonstrated that simulations play an important role in design problem solving" (p. 396). A model, simulation, or prototype plays the role of a "transitional object," helping the designer to learn and to change their understanding of what something is and how it works. The term "transitional object" was coined by Seymour Papert and colleagues at the Tavistock Institute to represent how in the process of playing with a model of the real world, children change their understanding of the world. By playing with and exploring their world through models, children "transit" into the next phase of development (Papert, 1980). Just as a designer or a child sometimes needs to be able to visualize, touch, and play with a prototype or model in order to solve a problem or to stimulate their thinking, strategy innovators can benefit from being able to visualize and play with a strategy, a decision, or an idea. Simon (1981) also suggested simulations can be used to help us better understand systems. They can be a source of new knowledge and can be used to help us predict the behavior of poorly understood systems.

Morecroft and Sterman (1994; Morecroft, 1992) discussed how the process of building models is itself a valuable learning process for managers. As a team of executives shares their mental models about the world in which they operate, and begin to operationalize their assumptions about the relationships between variables, the team ultimately arrives at a shared model of the business and its environment. This collective shared model is almost always much richer, more sophisticated, and more complete than any one individual's prior mental model of the business and its environment. The result of this process is a formal mathematical model incorporating the rich understanding of an experienced group of senior executives. Once such a model is developed, the executive team can use it to rehearse, visualize, and test different strategic options (Morecroft, 1984, 1999).

Research illustrates that people cannot accurately predict the consequences of complex system dynamics such as temperature and climate changes (Sterman and Sweeney, 2002), or deduce the consequences of the interacting components underlying organizational operations or strategy (Morecroft, 1984, 1999; Sterman, 1989). This is where computer modeling of strategy can provide valuable support acting as a prototype or "transitional object" helping strategy developers to learn, and challenging their understanding of their problems and decisions. A strategy model can also help developers visualize and understand the implications of their decisions, and how those decisions interact with each other and the external environment. Strategy models help strategy developers by making strategy visible and by keeping track of the complexity of interacting relationships that our minds cannot (Stiles, 2006). Strategy models provide strategy developers with

> effective graphic display methods for illustrating the policy structure of an organization...they can see the range of interlinked policies that constitute their organization. They can see the complex network of communication and control through which strategy initiatives must filter to bring about change in organizational performance. (Morecroft, 1984, p. 217)

Stiles (2006) suggested computer simulations can help managers from the shop floor make production decisions and help strategists decide if mergers or partnerships would pay off and how well. For example, the use of strategy models in a case outlined by Morecroft (1984) illustrated how it gave strategy developers insight into the subtle and complicated interrelationships between the size, productivity, and motivation of the sales force, sales levels, market share, and product price. Strategy developers realized, for example, that sales force reductions could precipitate a spiral of declining productivity, motivation, and market share. This is relatively easy to understand. However, the use of the model also illustrated the counterintuitive fact that significant increases in the sales force size also reduced market share because the resultant rise in customer awareness not only led to more sales for their organization but it also led to increased sales for a competitor. This new understanding of the complex interactions involved brought into question the desirability of a rapid conversion of existing customers from old products to new offerings as a goal in its own right, and led to further work on combination changes in sales force size and product price (Morecroft, 1984).

As we have seen, prototyping helps designers, and can help strategy innovators, generate and explore various ideas and possibilities. It helps designers reduce risk and helps make ideas visible. Prototyping strategy via computer modeling can be a valuable tool helping strategy innovators do the same.

CHAPTER SIX

Evaluation and Refinement

Up to this point in the process designers have deliberately avoided evaluation. They have been concerned mainly with divergent thinking as their goal has been to be creative and to generate and explore as many different ideas as possible. At some point in the process, however, it becomes necessary to move from divergent to convergent thinking as they start refining solutions, limiting options, making decisions, and reaching conclusions.

> I spend some time ideating and sketching, gradually focussing on the designs I believe are the strongest. Those concepts are then reviewed with marketing, sales, design and engineering—this proves the viability of the concept, and helps narrow down the concepts to the best candidates. I then refine the most well-received ideas, and perhaps one or two of my personal favorites, and I present them to senior management for final selection. (Anthony, Industrial Designer)

Evaluation is a critical part of the action learning cycle wherein we trial something, we evaluate, observe, and learn from the results, incorporate the insights and learning into something better that we trial, and we continue to cycle around. Developmental evaluation is a continual process of refinement, not a specific point in time. Prototyping plays a significant role in this refinement process for many designers. Prototyping is simultaneously an evaluative process, part of the creative development cycle, and part of the output and transfer process as well.

According to Kimbell, Stables, and Green (1996) the purposes of this evaluation stage in the design process are to judge or make decisions about aspects of the design as it develops, and to reflect on the strengths and weaknesses of the design once completed. "This final phase is indispensable to any creative project...we must call upon our own judgement and the judgement of others to verify— not only to assay our final findings, but also at intermediate stages, for such purposes as to focus objectives, and to call out hypotheses" (Osborn, 1953, p. 180).

We, therefore, see that evaluation has two aspects to it. One is a refinement aspect as it is part of the ongoing iterative cycle of development. The second aspect is terminal, focused on judging whether or not something meets specified criteria or choosing from among alternatives. Consider the following example in which we see illustrations of both of these aspects of evaluation in the design process:

> We have one of the most extensive evaluation systems of any museum in the country [The Powerhouse (Science and Technology) Museum, Sydney Australia]. We evaluate the idea with a series of focus groups, different age groups, different socio-economic and clientele groups, to test first of all whether or not the idea works. Often we will change the idea because of that. The next thing we do is a prototype of a number of the elements. We prototype some interactive pieces or the way we are presenting material, and we test to see if that is working. After the exhibition is constructed we do an evaluation of the visitor. We track people as they go through an exhibit and we sometimes stop them and ask them questions. Once you have tracked 20 or 30 people, you have tracked how the majority of people will move through the exhibition. And finally we look at did we get the numbers of visitors and did we get the reactions we wanted. We do a lot of evaluation to help us try and understand our audience. (Brad, Museum Design Manager)

Strategy developers do a great deal of evaluation, but according to the designers' view of the world, they seem to evaluate the wrong things and to do it too early in the process. Designers, as we have seen, tend to try and hold-off on evaluation, and focus on creativity, exploration, and on generating many varied options at the start, while strategy developers tend to start the process with evaluation and with trying to find the one "right" or best answer before they put much serious effort in to an idea. At the later stages in the strategy development process, traditional strategy developers do little developmental evaluation as they have already made their decisions by then, and are focused more on implementation and execution. It is not at all common for various strategic options to continually be sent through a developmental refinement feedback loop. Revisiting a strategic choice or option is more likely to be seen as a sign of problems, or of outright failure, than as part of a developmental refinement process within a larger creative process of strategy innovation by design.

It is, however, a requirement for successful innovation that we continue to learn, evolve and develop. For example,

> great designers continue to modify and enhance the design after it's in use rather than insisting that it be cast in stone. For many, Apple's iPod is the current poster child for perfect design—elegant, intuitive, delightful, economical, etc. However the iPod went through a lengthy period of profound design changes after its first launch to become the "instant success" that everybody thinks it is (as chronicled by former chief scientist for Alias Wavefront Bill Buxton in a forthcoming book on design). Without Apple's willingness to keep modifying and enhancing the iPod, even though it was already successful, we wouldn't have the marvelous current manifestation or the likely further enhancements that we may not yet be able to contemplate. (Martin, 2005b)

For strategy to be successful we need to do several things: we must (1) make decisions about what we will and will not do; (2) make a commitment of resources to a limited range of activities; (3) organize to do it; and (4) adapt, reinvent, and iteratively develop as we get feedback from the market and from those responsible for its execution. Our traditional technocratic strategy formulation methods are focused on the first two or three requirements (Daniell, 2004; Henderson, 1979; Johnston and Bate, 2003; Porter, 1996; Rughase, 2006; Simons, 2005). They rarely ever consider the fourth element of adaptation, reinvention, and iterative development. It is this final stage, however, that provides opportunities for learning and development, and turns the procedure into an iterative process of strategy innovation by design.

Strategy developers, therefore, can learn several things from designers about the evaluation stage of the strategy creation process. First, designers sometimes start by trying things out, they experiment and develop them over time, rather than always starting with analyses and decisions about what they will and will not do, or by focusing and making a commitment of resources to a limited range of activities up-front. Second, designers can teach strategy developers how to use prototypes and trials to better adapt, reinvent, and iteratively develop strategy as we get feedback from the market and from those responsible for its execution. Finally, strategy developers can learn the value of greater stakeholder involvement in the strategy development and evaluation process. In the remainder of this chapter, therefore, we will briefly distinguish between developmental and terminal evaluation. We will explore developmental evaluation via evaluative prototyping as well as terminal evaluation and the importance of both rational and nonrational evaluation methods. We will discuss participation and involvement in the evaluation process and the design process more generally.

Developmental and Terminal Evaluation

As just discussed, evaluation can be developmental, and focused on iterative refinement, or it can be terminal leading to a final choice or decision. If the goal is to learn, refine, play, and explore, developmental evaluation is the focus. If, however, the goal is to choose between alternatives, reach a "go" or "no-go" decision, or to systematically find flaws and problems in an idea, a terminal evaluation approach is likely necessary. The first step in the process, therefore, is to articulate the goals of the evaluation. Once we know what it is we are trying to achieve (i.e., developmental evaluation or terminal evaluation) we can then choose an appropriate evaluation process.

Developmental Evaluation: Evaluative Prototyping

At this developmental evaluation stage in the design process designers start to move away from their sole focus on creativity and exploration, and they start to focus also on convergent thinking: evaluating, refining, and detailing. We must remember, however, that this process requires both divergent thinking to generate the next round of improved creative alternatives, and convergent thinking to evaluate, identify the better options, further develop those, and plan their further development and eventual execution. Designers continually report that prototypes are essential tools enabling successful developmental evaluation (Boland and Collopy, 2004b; Brown, 2008; Erickson, 1995).

Of course [a decision] occurs after rounds and rounds of prototyping, and often after rounds of failure. (Alex, Industrial-Designer)

It is important sometimes to do quick checks and get small approvals from the client. Like a rapid prototyping. (Eberto, Architect)

The next thing we do is a prototype of a number of the elements. We prototype some interactive pieces or the way we are presenting material, and we test to see if that is working. (Brad, Museum Design Manager)

Design as a process is in the business of creating possible solutions rather than reducing avenues... You still wind up at the same place because we have a sense that option number three from our visualization and prototyping is probably going to be the one, but we now have a tangible solution-driven approach, whereas strategy consultants try to prove that certain angles of approach are pointless. (Andrew, Designer, Management Consultant)

Because design and strategy problems are often ill-defined, proposing many ideas and prototyping a number of solutions is sometimes the best means of understanding the problem and evaluating alternative options. With many types of complex problems, assumptions, constraints, and critical criteria are often only identifiable after we start proposing and exploring potential solutions (Camillus, 2008; Christensen, 2009; Conklin, 2006; Rittel and Webber, 1973). In other words, designers remind us that sometimes trial and error are inevitable as at the start, we do not always know what it is that we do not know. Consider the following light-hearted example of how the developmental evaluation of a solution via prototyping can uncover previously unthought-of and completely unexpected problems (Rubinstein and Hersh, 1984):

[We were] using prototype evaluation, a human factors technique, to uncover problems with a computer system design. The way the children were to interact with the computer was also novel: to answer questions, they used a light pen to point at things on the screen. One thing the evaluators learned from this study was that the children stuck the light pens in their ears, and the ear wax blocked the photocells so that the light pens couldn't detect light coming from the display screen. The systems could not be kept working! The designers of the system had never foreseen this problem. (p. 189)

In addition to uncovering the unexpected, developmental evaluation via prototyping helps us to explain and sell the strategy or ideas to others.

Getting something in 3-D, a prototype, is critical. Once they [the client] see it, you can see the look they have on their faces. They can relate more easily. (Catroina, Architect)

Even though design is no good at constructing logical arguments to generate buy in, design prototypes are unparalleled in their ability to generate enthusiasm. There is nothing quite as good as looking at something, touching it and seeing it, being made to believe it is real, this is not going to happen in two years time, this is today, now, it is here. (Andrew, Designer and Management Consultant)

Consider the following example from Brown (2005) that illustrates the power of a prototype to generate feedback and enable us to evaluate, learn, evolve, and further develop an idea or strategy, as well as to communicate a concept, and make it visual and real for people:

Some years ago, a startup called Vocera came to us with a new technology based on the Star Trek communicator—that "Beam me up, Scotty" device. They had worked out the technology—an elegant device the size of a cigarette lighter that you could wear around your neck and use to connect instantly with anyone on the network. But the team had no way to describe why people would need the thing. We made a five-minute film that played out a scenario where everyone in the company had these gadgets. The storyline followed how one person used the communicator to rapidly assemble a crisis team disbursed across an office campus. The film showed that while text communications and mobile phones are very good for expected interactions, this device was ideal for reacting to the unexpected.
    The team used the film to tell their story; it helped them raise the VC funding and it acted as the guiding framework for the development and marketing of the product, which is called the

Vocera Communications Badge. But there's an interesting twist to this tale. We thought the badge would work best on big office campuses. The market thought otherwise. Vocera's two largest markets are hospitals and big-box retail stores.

In the end, it didn't really matter that the market opportunity morphed into something different. Because you're testing and refining your strategy early and often in the design process, the strategy continually evolves. When the market changes, as it did with Vocera, the strategy can change along with it.

Even after you've rolled out your new product, service, or process, you're just getting started. In almost every case, you move on to the next version, which is going to be better because you've had more time to think about it... The market is always changing; your strategy needs to change with it. Since design thinking is inherently rooted in the world, it is ideally suited to helping your strategy evolve. (p. 54)

We can see, therefore, that developmental evaluation via prototyping is essential in a fast-moving complex word for designing new products, services, solutions, and strategies.

Terminal Evaluation: The Head and the Heart

Of course, at some point we reach the time when alternatives must be evaluated, and a decision made regarding how to proceed. So, how do designers decide when something is done? When is an idea, a product, or a solution considered to be beautiful, perfect, priceless, or "ready to go"? There are a number of terminal evaluation methods that seem to be popular with designers. They can be classified simply into two categories: rational methods and nonrational methods.

Proponents of rational evaluation methods remind us that all the rational decision-making tools that are available to managers can be applied to the evaluation of a design. There are many individual and group voting methods that can be used, as well as methods for the formal testing of prototypes, and the use of formal decision matrices wherein each concept is rated against weighted, specified selection criteria and a score is calculated. The product or design that is shown, via rational, quantitative analysis methods to optimize communication, route efficiency, and cost minimization, or is considered most likely to make more money is most efficient regarding space and/or energy utilization, is the safest, the one that best meets the prespecified criteria, or the one that is most consistent with the goals and objectives outlined in the brief can be chosen relatively objectively and rationally (cf. Cross, 2000; March, 1976; Rainey, 2005; Ulrich and Eppinger, 2004). Rainey (2005) provided an excellent chapter on rational design validation and evaluation methods. In it, he discussed several internal, external, and risk evaluation methods. He reminded us that product testing, market testing, operational, production/delivery testing, financial testing, supply-networks testing, related-industries testing, infrastructure testing, competitive analysis, and risk and uncertainty assessment (market-related risk, technical risk, program-related risk, stakeholder risk, and financial risk) are all potentially important for the rational evaluation of designs. According to Cross (2000) "In fact, the evaluation of alternatives can only be done by considering the objectives that the design is supposed to achieve." In other words, the success of a design must be assessed in relation to its brief (Bernstein, 1988; Boyle, 2004). The brief is often considered the ultimate yardstick from this rational design evaluation perspective.

Proponents of the nonrational evaluation methods, however, suggest that it is intuition that plays the major role in the design decision and evaluation process. The design, solution, or idea might be chosen because it feels right and seems better to people on the team (Ulrich and Eppinger, 2004).

I always have a personal choice or favourite. I often give two choices, my personal choice and a safer option. (Joel, Graphic and Communications Designer)

Evaluation is instinctual and about aesthetics, strength of design. If I can get lost in it, boldness and narrative, use of color and space, the juxtaposition of something bold and subtle. (Simon, Illustrator, Graphic Designer)

I trust my gut. People who are not directly involved in the creative process often have a hard time understanding this because there is no formula. There is no list of check boxes to fill out that will tell you if you have a good product or not. I also trust the guts of my peers. Some people have a good product sense, others don't. I try to find the ones that do and see what they think...in the end trust your gut! (Alex, Industrial-Designer)

While some designers think that evaluation should be completely rational, and others consider it an intuitive process, the vast majority of designers seem to think it is a two-stage process involving both the head (i.e., rational, objective) and the heart (i.e., nonrational, intuitive). When designers talk about evaluation, and choosing the best design from among several options on the table, they often discuss using both their objective and their subjective sides, assessing both function and form, and making sure the design or solution both works and is beautiful or aesthetically pleasing. In other words, they evaluate holistically using a combination of both their rational and intuitive sides.

The best design can be determined by several factors. When you have the right design everything just comes together. It functions well and looks good. When you hold it, you can feel the quality. When you see it, nothing about it bothers you and when you use it, it works smoothly. (Kacie, Industrial Designer)

I use a filtering process. First, does it meet my criteria and the client's brief? This is the first filter. The second filter is subjective, do I like it; does it feel right? (Alison, Physical Work Environment Designer)

I do evaluation via function, aesthetics and efficiency. (Charles, Architect)

Evaluation is done based upon number one functionality, then aesthetics, and number three sustainability in terms of flexibility and long-lasting. (Jorge, Design Educator)

Evaluation for a house or a private client...first I compare the designs to the brief and the requirements, then I look at some less tangible aspects and I feel into a place, into the context. (Chris, Architect)

Is it appropriate for the target, does it work, and is it beautiful? (David, Graphic Designer and Educator)

I compare the outcome to the objectives, and use my intuition. (Ron, Visual Communication Designer)

The best designs are when the finished product, form or service directs or informs the intended function, and at the same time inspires the manifestation of higher and more evolved functions. (John, Architect, Management Consultant and Coach)

When I choose there is always a favourite. One is at 34% and the other two choices are at 33%. I might check with a friend. There is usually one option that is obviously, objectively, better. It works better, it is more functional, is the most pragmatic, the most successful, uses the least energy... I trust a lot of my instincts too so, yes you need to be really rational about it but you also need to let the emotions kick in. (Eberto, Architect)

Evaluation is always done by comparison to the brief. Clients needs are in the brief. You have to ask does it meet those requirements. And second, it's more subjective, is it professionally presented? Is it beautiful? (Rod, Illustrator and Design Educator)

Evaluation is always related to satisfying the brief. Then I look for the most innovative, something I have not seen before or something that challenges or excites me. (Kay, Interior Designer)

The first question I ask is about purpose; does the design answer the brief and fulfil its criteria? Then I look at form, composition and balance. First, does it meet the criteria, and then does it do more, is there a back story, a rationale? (John, Media Designer)

Evaluation has a formal side to ensure it meets the needs of the client and the marketplace, and an informal side which is did the client like it, is it innovative, value-added, does it have a creative kick? (Robert, Product Designer, Design Educator)

Evaluation is intuitive and holistic, and you have to consider how it satisfies the criteria given. (Todd, Interior Designer, Design Educator)

Evaluation is first asking the question did the design answer the brief. The second thing is recall ability and memorability, the impact it has on you, is that appropriate to the target market? And third, is a pleasing to the eye, is it good visual communication? I look at beauty and line. (Lynda, Graphic Designer, Book Designer)

Evaluation is from a functional point of view primarily. Is it capable to do what it is supposed to? Then we look at the more artistic side, does it have emotion and the right sort of angles? Putting those together is what separates fine art from design. When you get both sitting side-by-side you have something that hums. (Richard, Graphic and Digital Multimedia Designer)

The design literature also supports this notion of design evaluation as the synthesis of the beautiful and the functional, the symbolic and the utilitarian, the numerically optimal or best, and that which has order, symmetry, beauty, and harmony. For example, Liedtka (2000) suggested that the concept of synthesis—the creation of a coherent harmonious whole emerging with integrity from a collection of specific design choices—constitutes the earliest and most fundamental notion of what good design is. Steiner (2005) suggested that criteria for workspace evaluation should consider both objective/rational elements such as space utilization per work-station, flexibility, and ergonomics and health, as well as less tangible factors such as how inspiring or motivational the workspace design was to users. According to Friedman (2002), designers integrate the scientific and the sensual, the intellectual and the intuitive. Norman (2004) suggested the bottom-line with any design is how it engages us viscerally, behaviorally, and reflectively, interweaving both emotions and cognition, providing both meaning and value. In Dreyfuss' (1955/2003) classic work on designing for people, he discussed the following five criteria for design evaluation. The first three are more rationally objective, while the fourth and fifth are more subjective: (1) utility and safety, (2) maintenance, (3) cost, (4) sales appeal, and (5) appearance. Finally, Brown (2008) suggested, "Great design satisfies both our needs and our desires . . . [they] appeal to us emotionally and functionally. In other words, they do the job and we love them" (p. 92).

The quintessential example of holistic design evaluation was proposed by Papanek in his classic book (1971) on design for the real world. He suggested a design be judged on how well it fares in terms of the integration of the soft and hard, the feeling and thinking, and the intuitive and intellectual across each of the following six aspects:

1. Method. Optimal use in terms of efficiency and cost. Never trying to make the material seem that which it is not.
2. Association. The appropriate association of things within a cultural context, as opposed to the mis-association of status with gimmickry.
3. Aesthetics. A tool that helps in shaping form and color so that it is meaningful and beautiful, moving and pleasing.
4. Need. Design should fulfil genuine human needs, not passing, superficial wants and desires.
5. Telesis. Context and culture must be considered so things seem to fit in.
6. Use. Does it work? Use must also be reasonable and appropriate.

Finally, Papanek (1984) suggested that the ultimate evaluative yard-stick is elegance. This provides a more concise and simple criterion that embodies the original six and goes beyond them.

> That's the elegance of it, that it actually stopped at the right point; it didn't elaborate, or it didn't go too far, or it wasn't over embel-lished, like the glass bottle for the Coco Chanel Number Five classic perfume. I mean that's a classic bottle, it's lasted. Now, that's design isn't it? . . . People understand its beauty, and it's priceless in a way. (Angelo, Architect)

> When I evaluate I ask "will it become an icon?" Even if it does not sell well as a design, if it influences others, other designers, it cas-cades and has a great effect. (Gabriele, Design Historian, Design Critic)

Strategy developers can recognize elegance as well as any other group of people when they come upon it. Unfortunately, the evaluation processes and tools used by strategy developers are almost exclusively rational and are not likely, therefore, to produce elegance. Within the strategy texts I examined (see chapter one), they virtually all focused on rational analyses of aspects of the external and internal environments as the only means of evaluating and choosing a strate-gic direction. In Porter's (1980) classic book on competitive strategy for example, he solely discussed rational evaluation methods such as ranking and summarizing data, comparing and analyzing competi-tor's financial results, and estimating competitors' cost curves and rel-ative costs. As one would expect, in traditional strategy development literature there are few conversations about the need for evaluation by both the head and the heart leading to the production of iconic elegance.

Involvement in Evaluation

So far in this chapter, we have seen that designers often begin the pro-cess by experimenting and developing ideas over time, rather than start-ing with analyses and assuming that final evaluation decisions should follow immediately. We have also discussed briefly how designers use prototypes to help iteratively evaluate and develop ideas, and how that is rarely ever part of the traditional strategy development process. A third thing strategy developers can learn from designers regarding evaluation is the value of engaging stakeholders actively in the process of developing and narrowing their choices.

Most designers believe that for successful design and innovation to occur, customers and employees should be involved in several aspects of the process. Several design-related involvement methods (e.g., participative design, usability testing, and user-centered design) have been shown, across a diverse range of applications, to be effective in increasing the success (e.g., user acceptance, learning, efficiency, satisfaction, performance, and quality) of the design of buildings and workplaces (Davies, 2004), of websites (Baek and Lee, 2008; Bordac and Rainwater, 2008; Dowding and Johnson, 2008; Manzari and Trinidad-Christensen, 2006; Park, 2008), of human computer interaction (Vaughan et al., 2007), of urban plans (Crewe, 2001), of postgraduate trainees during their residency in a child and adolescent psychiatry program (Davis et al., 2009), and of the development of scientific software (Macaulay et al., 2009).

Many of those interviewed also highlighted the importance for successful design of broad involvement in several phases of the design process:

When I start the design process I always use participatory design... [and] evaluation must be a group effort. Workshop the evaluation with representatives from all possible communities and concerns. (Filippo, Product and Process Designer)

It's definitely not an easy process and everybody has to be involved. (Eberto, Architect)

The user experience makes the difference between a quality product and one that was made with little thought. Since the quality is defined by the user, the elements you design change according to the customer's values. (Kacie, Industrial Designer)

In our office we do reviews of the projects constantly... It's [done] to pick up stupid things you may have done, why would you, for example, put a hand basin of that size in a bathroom when the bathroom is so big? You know reviews pick up things that as designers we miss and so you need to have many people in that review process. (Julia, Architect)

Once your research is done, the best way to evaluate the solution is to find three or four concepts that you feel, based on your research, will be a good solution. These concepts can be further

refined by having mockups made and then tested on the end user
to evaluate customer reaction. From those concepts, we can then
move to finalize the design of the one. (Jim, Industrial Designer)

According to the design literature, the more involvement you have from
stakeholders, the better the ultimate solution is likely to be (Baskerville
and Stage, 1996; Binder and Brandt, 2008; Eason, 1997). Liedtka (2000)
and Dodgson, Gann, and Salter (2005) have all suggested participation
is critical for successful design as it produces a collective learning that simultaneously educates individuals and shapes the evolving choices. Martin
(2005b) holds that every person in an organization, from the chief
executive at the top of the hierarchy to the customer-service representative at the bottom, is a choice-making brain, and should be involved
in both strategy formulation and implementation.

I find the client, more often than not, wants to be a designer
or wants to be lead through the design process, and working on
this baby food company job I found that they were more receptive to our ideas if we made them part of the design process, and
then made them feel as if the decisions were their ideas. (Julia,
Architect)

Evaluation must be collaborative. Engineers are always involved
in the design process with designers, and the whole is then greater
than the sum of the parts. (Philip, Industrial Designer)

Of course, the strategy development and evaluation process can and
sometimes does involve employees as well as customers/clients, external
consultants, and/or some other stakeholders. Traditionally, however,
strategy development and evaluation processes are the sole purview
of senior managers (Beall, 2001; Clarke, Butcher, and Bailey, 2004;
Le Theule and Fronda, 2005; McCullagh, 2006). Rarely does strategy
development involve more than a handful of an organization's most
senior managers (cf. Hamel, 1998). I asked 165 managers from a broad
range of industries about who was involved in strategy development in
their organizations. Of them, 52 percent (86) said only senior managers
were involved and 45 percent (75) said it was a mix of senior managers and a few key others. Only 2 percent (4 people out of 165) said
that there was broad representation in the strategy development process
from across the organization.
    This is an important issue for the creation of strategy innovations.
Several authors in the strategy field have suggested that involving

stakeholders in the development and evaluation process leads to greater buy-in and commitment, which will lead to greater effort and, therefore, more successful implementation, while it also leads to greater diversity of inputs and, therefore, better quality decisions in the first place. For example, DiVanna and Austin (2004) discussed the benefits of a diversity of inputs to strategy formulation in terms of the quality of the strategy developed and risk reduction. Collier, Fishwick, and Floyd (2004) surveyed more than six thousand managers and concluded that involvement in the strategy development process led to more positive attitudes about the process, and made it more effective. Riis, Dukovska-Popovska, and Johansen (2006) suggested that an appropriate degree of participation in strategy development helps ensure ideas and ownership are gained from those who will be involved in its implementation. McKenna (2002) also called for broader involvement in the development of strategy suggesting it would lead to more successful development and implementation. Finally, in the health care industry in the United Kingdom, Carney (2004a,b, 2007) has illustrated that participation in strategy development leads to higher levels of motivation and commitment, higher levels of strategic consensus, and the development of better strategy.

In terms of involvement and participation in the evaluation process, therefore, we see that strategy innovation designers must begin by experimenting and iteratively developing ideas over time, with less of a focus on analyses and immediate final evaluation decisions. We see that strategy innovators should use prototypes and simulations to help iteratively evaluate and develop ideas. Finally, we see that in order to develop and implement strategy innovations successfully, we must engage stakeholders actively in the process of initially developing and later narrowing-down choices.

CHAPTER SEVEN

Delivery: Output and Presentation

We have reached the final phase of the design process. In this chapter we will consider how designers communicate their designs and solutions, and what strategy innovators can learn from them. Of course, designers use a great range of techniques to present their output. They use sketches, drawings, charts, plans, pictures, models, videos, scenarios, prototypes, storyboards, collages, specifications, variation orders and instructions, and other forms of output all delivered in a range of ways (e.g., formal meetings, informal meetings, inspections, design reviews, presentations, written reports and more; cf. Brown, 2007; Emmitt, 2002; Zachman, 1999). Regardless of the form, the defining characteristic of design output is that it is visual, and designers are focused on making their output real and tangible for people so it is better understood, more memorable and persuasive.

Visualization and Realization

When presenting solutions or strategy innovations to stakeholders, whether they are employees, the board, senior managers, clients, or customers, we must remember that the design team has been working on the formation and development of the solution or strategy for weeks if not months. Most likely, when the output is presented to other stakeholders, it is the first time they have heard about it in any detail. If the solution, product, or strategy is innovative, it will likely be perceived as unusual or different by many, and that means risky to some. Therefore, we need to take the audience on a journey; take them through a shortened or stylized version of the design process that has generated the output they are seeing. We can not just drop a radical idea on stakeholders and say, "OK, what do you think?" If we do this, the only thing we will know for sure is that whatever they will be thinking will not be what we are thinking.

To help ensure stakeholders will be able to understand and appreciate the value of design output, Drewniany and Jewler (2008) suggested beginning the design presentation process with a recap of the assignment, reminding the client of the problem, and sharing the creative exploration of it. It is important to share both ideas that were rejected as well as those that were built upon to form the final output. Drewniany and Jewler (2008) suggested discussing the creative process and output thoroughly, and being sure to link the output clearly to the goals of the project.

The way designers help ensure that their output will be memorable and persuasive, as well as understood and appreciated, is that they make it visual and real for stakeholders. Many of the designers interviewed discussed the importance of visualization to the design process and design output.

When visual concept drawings and non-working prototypes wouldn't do, we persuaded the top management of Motorola to pursue the Family Radio Service (FRS) consumer walkie talkie business category in the following way: We created fifty working pairs of radios and gave them as gifts to top management. They used these consumer two-way radios while on the ski slopes, hiking, biking, etc. In this case the value of the product had to be experienced. Management later initiated the program and it grew to be a $1,000,000 business within 2 years. In a separate instance, my high resolution computer renderings of a medical concept were added to a government grant proposal that had been declined three times previously. The removal of text in favor of design imagery resulted in two SBIR government grants for $500,000 each proving that a picture is worth a thousand words, and in this case one million dollars in funding. (Frank, Industrial Designer)

Visualization is central. If you can't see it you can't make it. (Rod, Illustrator and Design Educator)

Visualization is extremely important. That is how I make my living 'cause most people can't do it. People need to see things to be sure they know what they mean. (Dave, Consumer Product Designer)

Visualization is paramount. There are two types of people, those who can visualize and those who can't. I have to be able to project the finished piece in my mind and see it from different angles, and I have to communicate it to the client. If you cannot visualize it you can not communicate it. (Dave, Fine Jeweller)

Output presentations include plans, sketches, multidimensional impact analysis and verbal scenarios. (John, Architect, Management Consultant and Coach)

In a typical process, designs may be presented in loose two-dimensional sketches in early efforts, and progress to higher degrees of fidelity such as tight renderings, computer renderings, videos, or even highly developed models as time and budget allow. Everything is always presented in context reflecting back to the original mission and strategy we have developed. Otherwise, it is fine art. Fine art is only good for three people: one, the artist; two, the artist's best friend; and three, the person that writes a check for it. That's not very effective to develop driver products to suit a wide audience. (Brian, Industrial Designer)

I do not work visually, I live visually. I always want to know why I remember the one image out of the 35,000 images I see in a day. (Lynda, Graphic Designer, Book Designer)

Designers are so visually focused that on the cover of the 540-page, four-inch-thick, *A-Z of Modern Design* (Polster et al., 2004) the selling point on the front cover are the "Over 2800 illustrations" that are advertised to be in it. Brown (2007) discussed the ten most common web design deliverables (e.g., personas that are a combination of character profiles and user scenarios, concept models, site maps, and flow charts that are all diagrams). All ten of them are designed to be visual or to make the output more real and accessible to the intended audience. Mair, Miller, and Anderson (2005) highlighted the importance of multimodal imaging and presentation to good design. They suggested using not just the visual mode (e.g., color, form), but also the aural (sound), olfactory (smell), kinesthetic (perception or sensing of the motion, weight, or position of the body as muscles, tendons, and joints move), and tactile (touch) modes wherever possible to enhance the experience of the end product, solution, or design.

Two related methods that designers use to help make their output more visual, accessible, and real are story-telling and scenario creation.

It is all about narrative, character and story, even with images. (Simon, Illustrator, Graphic Designer)

My background is in industrial design, but I am now heavily involved in art direction, animations and storytelling, and I use my industrial design problem-solving skills and apply them to my current work. (Jim, Industrial Designer)

I think when you're looking at the design in a more holistic way, you're looking at much more generalized sort of themes, so I tend to look at it in colour fields like a story generally has a colour mode that runs through it, so you take that into consideration when you see the story coming after it. So, you know, it's a dark story and then you seem to go for a light one and then you sort of try and make sure it's got a nice flow. (Shane, Communications Designer)

Scenarios can effectively tell a story and describe how social, technological, market, competitive, or other trends might influence people's behavior and the use of a product/service, solution, or environment (Anggreeni and van der Voort, 2008; IDEO Cards; Rosson and Carroll, 1995). Scenarios can show how a variety of people use a product, service, or industry in different ways and how different solutions can meet their needs (Nussbaum, 2004). These can take the form of textual narratives, storyboards, videos, prototypes, or physical situations depicting an experience or how the design might be used (Carroll, 1995; Johnson, Johnson, and Wilson, 1995). If you want to get feedback from a number of people on an idea, or if you want to communicate an abstract idea or situation, making the experience easier for people to visualize and remember by telling a story can help make it more real for them. Fluharty (2004) suggested that designers are skilled storytellers and have a gift for imagining and creating.

Storytelling and scenarios are, of course, not new to the world of business or strategy (cf. Hattersley, 1997; McKee, 2003; Swap et al., 2001; Wiles, 2003). A big part of a senior executive's job is to motivate people to reach goals, and the key to successfully doing this is to engage people both mentally and emotionally. One of the easiest ways to engage people and win their hearts and minds is to tell a story.

Stories are visual, and are often easier to remember than verbal information, lists, and bullet points (Kazui et al., 2003; McKee, 2003; Swap et al., 2001). For example, Green and her colleagues (Green, 2007, 2008; Green and Brock, 2000; Green, Brock, and Kaufman, 2004; Green et al., 2008) have theorized that "transportation into a narrative world" is a psychological mechanism through which stories affect beliefs. Their studies suggest "transportation," or absorption into a story, affects emotional responses, mental imagery, focus of attention, and cognitive focus. "Transportation" has been shown to lead to belief change in a variety of settings as it reduces the likelihood of counterargument, evokes strong emotions that are more likely to affect behavior, and makes the story seem more real. "The rich detail and concrete information in stories helps individuals remember the story, and also makes story events more influential" (Green, 2008, pp. 47–48). This is why design output, and strategy innovation output, must be made visual and tangible.

According to McKee (2003),

> there are two ways to persuade people. The first is by using conventional rhetoric, which is what most executives are trained in. It's an intellectual process, and in the business world it usually consists of a PowerPoint slide presentation in which you say, "Here is our company's biggest challenge, and here is what we need to do to prosper." (p. 52)

We then provide statistics, facts, and authoritative quotes and we expect to logically persuade our audience. The problem is that many people in the audience have their own sets of equally valid and persuasive statistics, facts, and experiences that logically lead them to a different conclusion. And even if we do succeed in persuading some of them, we have only done so intellectually and temporarily. This is frequently not enough to inspire people or to get them to change their behavior. The more powerful way to persuade people, according to McKee (2003) as well as Green and her colleagues (Green, 2007, 2008; Green and Brock, 2000; Green, Brock, and Kaufman, 2004; Green et al., 2008), is by telling a compelling story that unites an idea with an emotion.

Presenting Options

Another important question to consider regarding design output is whether it is better to present two or three options, involve the client/decision-maker, and engage them in the process by letting them discuss and/or choose from among the options, or is it better to present the "one" and hope those making the choice are satisfied. While not unanimous,[1] the vast majority of designers seem to think choice is the way to go as it better engages the client, helps increase their commitment and buy-in by giving them a chance to influence the design, and helps clarify communication (e.g., helps the client clarify what they really want, helps the client then communicate what they want to the designer, and helps the designer clarify that they understand what the client wants).

> Choice is important to give the client the sense they are making the decision. This way the client is involved. That is especially important early on. The designer takes more control later. (Rod, Illustrator and Design Educator)

> I definitely show them options, not to bamboozle them with choice, but to involve them from the beginning. (Simon, Illustrator, Graphic Designer)

> We have only done the "Ta-da!" thing once, where we presented the one-and-only concept. It worked but was really risky, and that client did not participate along the way very much. (Brian, Industrial Designer)

> It is important to allow the decision-maker some degree of influence, an opportunity to be involved in the outcome. It is simple human nature. The boss wants to proudly say to his or her friends and family, "That's my product." Therefore, the designer must know in advance what they are willing to give away in exchange for leading management to the right design decision. This could be as simple as inviting the decision maker to assist in selecting the product's color from a pallet of options the design team can live with. (Frank, Industrial Designer)

> With houses, we tend to show 2 or 3 optional design strategies as we find it a good way of clarifying a brief and clients, who are often clients for the very first time and are totally inexperienced, get a better chance of influencing the design process and collaborating with us, which we like. (Christopher, Architect)

> I give as many options as I can, depending on the job. Fewer options with websites, but with logos I give many choices. This

way the client can say "I like parts of options 1, 3 and 5. Can we bring them together?" This helps me try to get what is in their heads out. (Diana, Graphic Designer)

You most definitely give options. As a fine artist I get to choose, but working for a client as a designer they get to choose. I don't give a rubbish option; the bull's-eye is quite large so there are always multiple options to give them. I do not believe in my god-like ability. I advise them about what I think is the best, but they must be included in the decision. (Simon, 3-D Animator, Master Jeweller)

I never give only one option. The brief away specifies the need to provide two or three ruffs [rough sketches]. I take them through all three, they feel good to choose. (Lynda, Graphic Designer, Book Designer)

I may have three different concepts and several different varia-tions for each concept. It is good to give them a choice. We never give them only one option. (Joel, Graphic and Communications Designer)

I always produce three to five agreed upon options. That is in the brief. These are distinctly different designs, not variations of the same thing. (Dave, Consumer Product Designer)

This notion of giving three options is repeated often by designers. In fact, some designers use the three options quite tactically. They present one option that is safe or conservative, one that is more radical, and one that is somewhere in between.

I always give choice, never one that I would not be happy with. All three choices would be viable. I give one that is conservative, one from the mid range, and one more out there. I try and edu-cate the client to get them out of their comfort zone, and learn and grow. (John, Media Designer)

I always show three, I call it step, stretch, leap. In other words this is a step forward, we can do this easily. This next would require us to stretch our thinking and our capability; and finally this third idea is a leap, and the risk attached will offer equal reward. Even if there is a need to show nine variations of a design, I will still bucket them into step, stretch, and leap. (Mark, Industrial Designer)

I generally provide two or three ideas in practice that range from conservative to artistically inspired, or left field, and one in between. (Richard, Graphic and Digital Multimedia Designer)

So far in this chapter we have seen that designers often suggest it is best to present a few options and let stakeholders have some input into the final choice thus increasing their feelings of ownership and buy-in, rather than the designer picking the one right answer and then trying to sell it. With radical strategy innovation, it is important to take people along with you intellectually and emotionally on a journey of exploration and discovery, albeit a shorted version of it. This will help engage relevant stakeholders, help increase their commitment and buy-in, and help clarify what is in our and others' minds, and communicate this to each other. We have seen how some designers purposefully present a number of options that range from safe to more radical. Their idea is to educate the client and to prepare them to be able to consider more radical and innovative options. We have also seen that designers consider that their output must be visual and tangible so that it is more persuasive and memorable to stakeholders. These two points are critical for those of us concerned with radical strategy innovations because as we know, most strategy that is formulated is incremental and unless we manage the process well and make our output visual and, therefore, more real, understandable, memorable, and persuasive, it will continue to be so.

Paradigms of Design and Strategy Development

When presenting their solutions, designers draw from a repertoire of design paradigms. For example, Wake (2000) discussed ten design paradigms ranging from simple shapes to enclosures, bending and flexing, to more complex operations and relationships such as passages, objects within objects, attaching, and multifunctionality. These paradigms are important to designers as they provide approaches to solving design problems and novel ways of thinking about how things work by categorizing design knowledge and solutions. Designers can then draw on these fundamental approaches to solve the problems on which they are working. The obvious question for those of us concerned with the creation of strategy innovation is "What are the paradigms of strategy formulation, and can they provide approaches to solving problems and novel ways of thinking about how things work leading to successful strategy development?"

There are several authors who have discussed paradigms of strategic thought, strategic management, or strategy development. Mintzberg's ten schools of strategic thought, discussed in chapter one, would be obvious choices for the paradigms of strategy. However, there is great overlap between several of the schools and, therefore, there may be fewer than ten distinct paradigms. For example, there is as much in common between the design, planning, and positioning schools of thought as there is to distinguish between them. They are all prescriptive, they all assume the CEO is the strategic focal-point, and they are all exclusive in that only senior managers, and possibly experts and consultants, are involved in strategy formulation. They are focused on control, analysis, and the conception of explicit strategy that is fully formed before it is implemented. In fact, Mintzberg, Ahlstrand, and Lampel (1998) suggested, "the positioning school did not depart radically from the premises of the planning school, or even the design school" (p. 83). While these three views may be taken together as a rational analytical strategy development paradigm, the other seven schools they discussed defied all my attempts at meaningful subgroupings as they have little else in common besides being descriptive rather than prescriptive.

Cravens (1998) distinguished market-driven orientations [exemplified by Porter (1996) that draws heavily from strategic marketing segmentation, targeting, and positioning concepts] from the value, distinctive competency, and relationship views of strategic management. Oosthuizen (2000) once again distinguished the traditional positioning approach to strategy development from the complementary competency-based alternative, and the more dynamic and emerging real-time approach (akin to Mintzberg, Ahlstrand, and Lampel's emergent/learning view). Finally, we have the three approaches to strategy as outlined in Eisenhardt and Sull (2001). They suggested managers have three distinct competitive strategic choices: (1) position (build a fortress and defend it), (2) resources (nurture and leverage unique resources), and (3) simple rules (flexibly pursue fleeting opportunities; this is akin to Mintzberg's emergent and learning view).

It seems, therefore, that there are three distinct paradigms of strategy that are consistently referred to. The first is the traditional view, concerned with planning and positioning, focused on analysis of the external environment, and exemplified by Porter (1980, 1996). This positioning paradigm is distinctly different from the resource-based view of strategy that is more internally focused examining the role of idiosyncratic, immobile resources (Barney, 1991) and core competencies (Prahalad and Hamel, 1990) in creating competitive advantage.

The third distinct paradigm is the dynamic, real-time, iterative, trial-and-error-based emergent and learning view (Mintzberg and Waters, 1985; Mintzberg, Ahlstrand, and Lampel, 1998).

All three paradigms add significant value to our thinking and practice related to strategy development, and provide distinctly different approaches to solving problems, and novel ways of thinking about how strategy development works. For example, the positioning view helps us focus on what we will and will not do; it helps clarify the organization's value proposition, and also align the organization with its external environment. This consistency, or fit, helps prevent leakage of efforts, reduces coordination costs as it simplifies complex organizational interdependencies, provides barriers to imitation, and helps shape desired behavior. Unfortunately, while dominant, this paradigm still has some limitations and weaknesses. For example, its narrow analytical focus (Mintzberg, Ahlstrand, and Lampel, 1998) leads to a lack of flexibility and responsiveness to change, and its preoccupation with external analysis (Barney, 1991) leads to simplified considerations of critical internal factors.

The good news is that the second strategy development paradigm is strong where the first paradigm is weak, and vice versa. The value of the resource-based paradigm is that it helps us ensure we have the necessary resources, competencies, and capabilities to deliver our products/ services and execute our chosen position. It helps us decide who we should and should not hire. It helps us clarify our mission, vision, and values. It helps us arrange our resources internally to support and deliver value. Its weakness is that while we may be quite good at something, or have unique, inimitable, rare resources, there may be little need for them in the market-place. This is, of course, the strength of the positioning paradigm and why the two are complementary. Taken together, the outside-in positioning paradigm, and the inside-out resource-based paradigm form a virtuous cycle, each providing great value and filling-in where the other is weakest (see figure 7.1).

Unfortunately, both the inside-out resources-based paradigm and outside-in positioning paradigm together have some weaknesses and limitations. Because they are prescriptive, intended, and rational, they work best when the external environment is relatively stable and predictable, but less so when it is rapidly changing and ambiguous (Eisenhardt and Sull, 2001). It is difficult to communicate to everyone once a strategic position has been chosen and once it is implemented successfully, it is slow to change. Similarly, once unique, inimitable, valuable, and rare resources and competencies have been invested in, they are not easy to change, and people will not be motivated to let

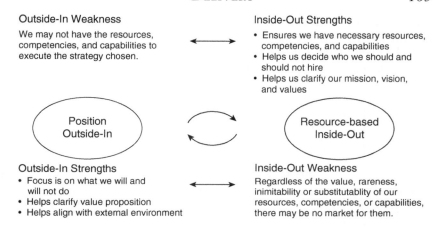

Outside-In Weakness

We may not have the resources, competencies, and capabilities to execute the strategy chosen.

Inside-Out Strengths

- Ensures we have necessary resources, competencies, and capabilities
- Helps us decide who we should and should not hire
- Helps us clarify our mission, vision, and values

Position
Outside-In

Resource-based
Inside-Out

Outside-In Strengths

- Focus is on what we will and will not do
- Helps clarify value proposition
- Helps align with external environment

Inside-Out Weakness

Regardless of the value, rareness, inimitability or substitutablity of our resources, competencies, or capabilities, there may be no market for them.

Figure 7.1   The virtuous cycle of the two prescriptive strategy development paradigms.

them go. Once again, the good news is that the third strategy paradigm, the emergent/learning paradigm, is strong where the first two are weak, and vice versa.

The strengths of the emergent/learning paradigm are its flexibility, allowing for adaptive, immediate responses to changes, and its ability to quickly seize opportunities and be successful in dynamic and ambiguous markets (Eisenhardt and Sull, 2001; Mintzberg, Ahlstrand, and Lampel, 1998). The limitations of the emergent/learning view are that we may look to the market like we do not have a strategy, and are unclear of our positioning and market-orientation, or at least cannot articulate what they are. We might find it difficult to plan and predict resource and capability needs as we do not know where we are going until we get there. Fortunately, the first two strategy paradigms are strongest in these areas of rational, formalized planning and control. In this way, the three paradigms once again form a virtuous cycle (as illustrated in figure 7.2) each providing great value and filling-in where the others are weakest.

As we have seen so far in this book, however, these three views even taken together still have some weaknesses and limitations. They are all focused on analysis of the past and/or the present, and are not good at helping us creatively invent a future. They are not focused on designing strategy innovations.

The strategy by design paradigm adds a fourth view of strategy development. It is different from the previous three as it is focused on creating an innovative future. It is a holistic combination of the rational and the intuitive, the head and the heart. It works best when the future must be created and cannot be predicted via analysis as a linear extension of the past or the present (see figure 7.3).

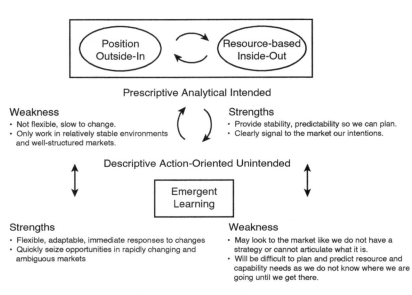

Figure 7.2 The virtuous cycle of the three strategy development paradigms.

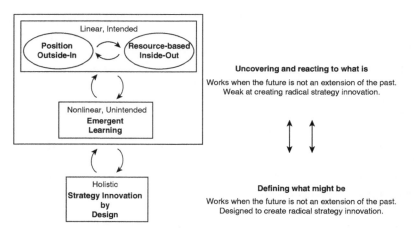

Figure 7.3 The virtuous cycle of the four strategy development paradigms.

Creating Strategy Innovations by Design

We asked these billion-dollar strategic questions at the start of the book: "How do we generate strategy innovations? How do we reinvent our organization, our industry, and our world?" As we have seen, strategy innovations do not already exist. They are not out there somewhere to be discovered via analyses. Strategy innovations must be designed.

The way to creatively generate strategy innovations by design is to start by defining our problem and establishing the brief. Do we want to address the problems of our dysfunctional financial system, alleviate hunger and poverty on the planet, or solve the problems related to greenhouse gases, global warming, and our biosphere at our world level, or do we want to reinvent the health care system or the air-travel industry, or do we want to generate a completely new business model that adds unprecedented value to all stakeholders, or radically reinvent our company and what it does?

Once we have an initial statement of the problem, we then question the most basic, obvious, and unquestionable assumptions and beliefs that we and others have related to the problem. We conduct research; we look, listen, try, and ask so we can better understand our stakeholders (e.g., customers) and identify their latent needs, and underlying values and functions related to the problem areas on which we are working. We use this information to go back and refine the brief ensuring we are asking the right questions. We conduct further research to help us better understand the problem and to explore creative ideas and potential solutions.

Once we have a relatively well-defined problem and brief, and we have conducted various forms of quantitative and qualitative research to gain insights into related aspects of the problem and the customer (or other relevant stakeholders), we then start to use all of this information, and our insights from our research, to help us generate many concepts and ideas related to potential solutions. We work hard, we apply the techniques of idea generation such as creative combination and alteration, random stimulation, identifying and violating assumptions, and others, so we can generate as many potential ideas and solutions as possible. We also allow time for incubation and for our more intuitive thinking processes to provide us with flashes of insight.

Then we begin to prototype, model, and pilot test several distinctly different avenues of solutions so we can explore and generate completely novel options, further changing and developing these based upon the feedback we get from others, and from our own experiences and experiments, until we reach the point of diminishing returns on this investment of our time and money. We eventually shift this focus from divergence and creativity to a focus on convergence as we begin to narrow down the options and possible solutions to those that are most promising. We evaluate our prototyped and modeled solutions using both our heads and our hearts, relying on rational, objective evaluation methods as well as subjective, intuitive methods to ensure economic viability and environmental sustainability, functionality, and beauty, and we constantly strive for elegant solutions that are the holistic combination of these two complementary sides.

Finally we present a small number of potential solutions in ways that are visual and that make them real for people to see, feel, touch, taste, and smell. This way, we have the best chance of designing and developing, appreciating and choosing, and then implementing successfully the most promising solutions and outcomes (see appendix for an integrated example of this entire process).

APPENDIX

An integrated example of the strategy by design process.

The design process and commentary	Redesigning the JIF Peanut Butter Factory in Lexington, Kentucky By Karen Lewis, College of Design, University of Kentucky
The brief, goal, problem	Initially, the idea was to redesign the factory.
Questioning the brief Instead of taking that as given and getting on with it, they questioned the brief and took a more holistic approach.	The students looked at the design of the JIF Peanut Butter Factory from two perspectives: the first was the process of making peanut butter and how that impacted the design of the factory; the second was to investigate the impact that the factory and the whole process of making peanut butter had on Lexington, Kentucky.
Questioning assumptions	They asked, "What was it like for neighbors to live near the factory, drive-by, and interact with it as an economic and industrial institution? Could the peanut butter factory be more than just the world's largest peanut butter factory, but rather the world's best factory?"
An idea worthy of pursuit	In considering these two questions, the studio challenged JIF to become more than just the world's largest peanut butter factory, but to be an institution that gave back to its community ecologically, economically, and culturally.
Research By looking at the wide scope of the peanut butter process, they were able to take a more holistic look at various aspects of the peanut butter making process, the factory, and the surrounding community.	Students started by researching and diagramming the entire peanut butter making process, from the growing and harvesting of peanuts, manufacturing, and finally distribution and marketing in the grocery store.

Continued

Continued

Traditional, background research	They identified that the JIF Peanut Butter Factory in Lexington, Kentucky, is the world's largest peanut butter factory. Every day, JIF produces approximately two hundred and fifty thousand jars of peanut butter, and processes more than seventy-seven billion peanuts each year.
Wide-ranging research of a number of related aspects of the problem with visual output. They look at the resources available and what other companies and institutions were available nearby.	They identified the steps in the peanut butter making process and created a Production Process Diagram (see example 1: The peanut butter production process map). They researched surrounding land uses and values, and produced a land value map (see example 2: Tha land value map) and several visual land value comparisons. They researched site activities and produced an activity map identifying high-use (darker) and low-use (whiter/lighter) areas (see example 3: An activity map).
Reformulation of the brief and the problem and creative combination	Students were asked to invent something—be it a new product, method, or system—that would bring two parts of the peanut butter production process together.
Concept generation; generate many ideas	One group considered the marketing and distribution aspects of peanut butter, and envisioned new RFID technologies to assemble custom-ordered peanut butter packages. Rather than a single case of crunchy and one of smooth, stores could tailor their orders based on local demographics. Another group suggested harvesting and shelling could be aligned, and proposed a new moisture-wicking peanut harvesting bag that would automatically shell peanuts as they were collected. Still others considered Peanut Butter and Community, Peanut Butter and Real Estate, and Peanut Butter and Social Condenser concepts.
Idea-generating exploratory research	The "Peanut Paper Project" explored how the "waste" of unused peanut shells could be used by JIF to produce a more sustainable peanut butter product. Currently, raw peanuts are transported to JIF by train several times a week. Peanuts are harvested and shelled on site in Georgia, Alabama, or Texas, where the waste shells are ground up and sold as animal bedding or added to feed. Instead of shelling the peanuts off-site, the Peanut Paper Project looked to see how JIF could use the wasted peanut shells.
Further idea-generating exploratory research, creative questioning	In their research, the studio found that peanut shells are 80 percent cellulose. Cellulose, when mixed with water, can be made into paper. Could JIF make its own labels from the peanut shells it ignores? Since 850 peanuts are needed to make one jar of JIF and only 13 peanut shells are needed to produce a standard-sized JIF label, what are there other uses for peanut paper by JIF or Lexington?

Continued

Continued

Further research and concept generation (creative linking of information)	Since the studio also examined the real estate surrounding JIF and considered its potential as a community institution, the Peanut Paper Project recognized JIF's relationship to other surrounding infrastructure. The train spur that brings peanuts to JIF passes by two other Lexington institutions: Lexmark, the international printing company, and the Herald-Leader, the local newspaper, are both located on this same train spur. The Peanut Paper Project suggested the potential to revitalize the underused train infrastructure in Lexington with a productive peanut shell loop. The project suggests that shelled peanuts arrive at JIF, which in turn sends the shells to Lexmark who will make the peanut paper. Lexmark, looking to expand its new paper and printing technologies, then sends the paper to the Herald Leader to print the JIF labels, as well as the newspaper. Using the remaining 837 peanut shells, the Herald Leader could print a 915-page daily paper for their entire circulation.
Prototyping; evaluation refinement; output presentation	The student's then began to envision the public presence of this peanut train loop, and in rendering these relationships, found a way to relate differing institutions, production methods, and economies across local and international businesses, and agricultural and technological innovations.
They prototyped and modeled the site (see example 4: The site model), Peanut Butter Circulation Conceptual Model (see example 5: Conceptual model of peanut butter circulation), produced the networking JIF from peanuts to paper visual (see example 6: Peanut paper proposal suggests a joint venture to make paper out of peanut shells between JIF, Lexmark, and the local newspaper), a site plan, (example 7: Site plan), and finally a collage and a perspective that are examples of visual scenarios, snapshots, or stories (see example 8: Perspectives: A collage).	

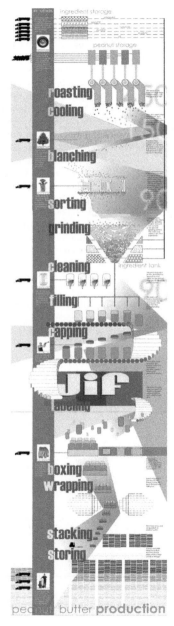

Example 1 The peanut butter production process map.

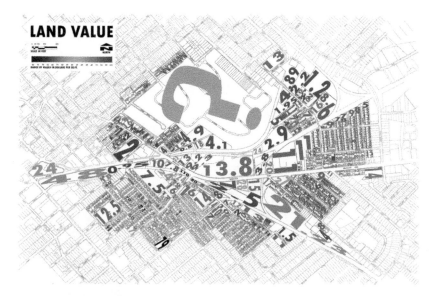

Example 2 The land value map.

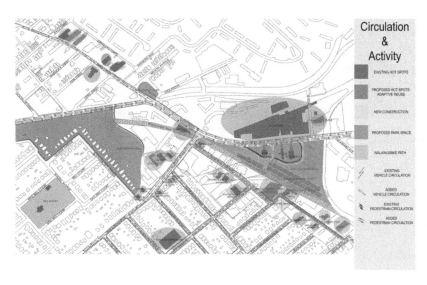

Example 3 An activity map.

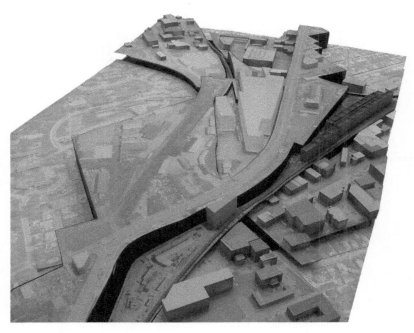

Example 4 The site model.

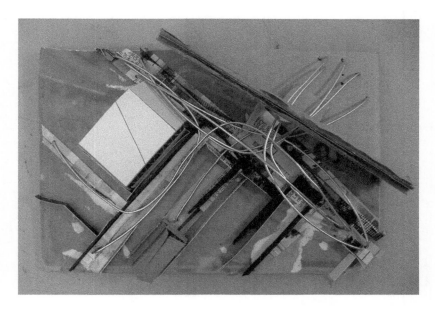

Example 5 Conceptual model of peanut butter circulation.

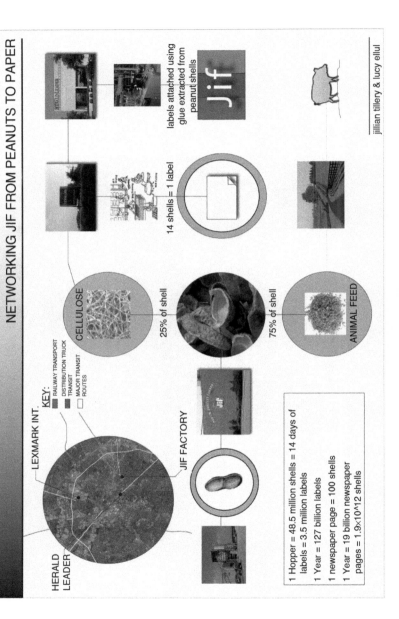

Example 6 Peanut paper proposal suggests a joint venture to make paper out of peanut shells between JIF, Lexmark, and the local newspaper.

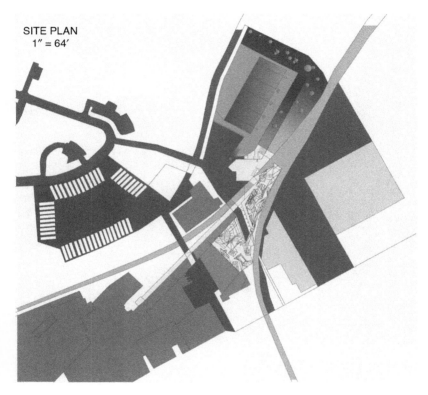

SITE PLAN
1″ = 64′

Example 7 Site plan.

Example 8 Perspectives: A collage.

NOTES

One   Strategy by Design: A Process of Strategy Innovation

1. I conducted interviews with over sixty designers (e.g., architectural, industrial, environmental, graphic, web, interior) from across the United States, Australia, and Europe. I will use quotes from these interviews throughout the book as illustrations of various points.
2. The modern design literature has a deep and rich history resting on the accomplishments of the likes of Benjamin Latrobe (1764–1820) who designed the U.S. Capitol Building and the porticoes of the White House, John Hall (1781–1841) who made good in 1824 on Eli Whitney's (1765–1825) 1798 promise to the U.S. government for the design, manufacture, and delivery of rifles/muskets with fully interchangeable parts, William Ware (1832–1915) who started the first architecture school in the United States in 1865 at the Massachusetts Institute of Technology, Louis Tiffany (1848–1933) of the famed Tiffany lamps and son of Charles Lewis Tiffany founder of Tiffany & Co, Norman Bel Geddes (1893–1958) who worked in theatrical design and is most noted for his work in industrial design related to aerodynamics and streamlining, Raymond Loewy (1893–1986) known for his fashion work for Vogue, Harper's Bazaar, Macys, and later for his industrial design work and his work for NASA, and Charles (1907–1978) and Ray Eames (1912–1988), the most notable couple in the history of the field of industrial design. Notable modern design publications start in the 1800s with works by Ruskin (1837/1838), Haweis (1878), and Day (1893) on architecture, aesthetics, design, and drawing, and continuing in to the 1900s with Pevsner's "Pioneers of Modern Design" (1936), Osborn's "Applied Creativity" (1953), Edel's "Introduction to Creative Design" (1967), Papanek's "Design for the Real World" (1971), Schutte's "The Uneasy Coalition" (1975), Archer and others (1979) in the first edition of *Design Studies* (a premier international peer reviewed journal for research in all fields of design), Cross (1982) on design thinking, and spreading more broadly through the social sciences and management literature through the work of such notables as Herbert Simon (1981) and Carl Weick (2003, 2004) who are more likely to be recognized by management scholars.
3. Examples of some of the many models of the high-level steps/phases in the design process are: inspiration, ideation, implementation (Brown, 2008); research, roughs, revise, ready, run (Drewniany and Jewler, 2008); pre-assessment, design (create prototype and distribute), assessment of prototype, revision of prototype, and repeat (McFall and Beacham, 2008); thinking, looking, doing (Lauer and Pentak, 2008); generating, synthesizing, selection, shaping (Zeiler and Savanovic, 2007); brief, research, concept generation, feedback, development, visualization/mock-up, to client (Kneeshaw, 2006); analysis, synthesis, evaluation

(Lawson, 2006); think, play, do (Dodgson, Gann, and Salter, 2005); analysis, design/ conceptualization, detailing/materialization (Liem, 2005); ideas, concept, definition, design, validation, pre-commercialization, and launch (Rainey, 2005); identifying, understanding, conceptualizing, realizing (Vogel, Cagan, and Boatwright, 2005); observation, brainstorming, rapid prototyping, refining (IDEO's design process from Nussbaum, 2004); development, design, technology analysis, requirements analysis, test, integration (Endsley, Bolte, and Jones, 2003); analysis, synthesis, appraisal, decision (Moughtin et al., 2003); identify the goal/wish/challenge, gather data, clarify the problem, generate ideas, select and strengthen solutions, plan for action (Osborn-Parnes Creative Problem Solving Cycle from Hughes, 2003); formulation, evolution, transfer, reaction (Press and Cooper, 2003); knowledge gain, preparation, incubation, stimulation, illumination (Bundy, 2002); discover, decide, deliver (Weiss, 2002); proposing, testing, adjusting, reformulating (Blyth and Worthington, 2001); problem identification and definition, analysis and observation, synthesis and reasoning, simulation and testing, evaluation and decision, acceptance or iteration (Whitbread, 2001); conception, creation, production, evaluation (Anders, 2000); observe context, investigate, develop ideas, refine, mock-ups, make, evaluate (Davis et al., 1997); investigate, plan, model/ make, design, evaluate (Kimbell, Stables, and Green, 1996); exploration, refinement, transition (Erickson, 1995); information design, interaction design, presentation design (Satran and Kristof, 1995); clarify parameters of the problem, explore the problem and examine possibilities, propose tentative solution, try solution out against the initial problem, redesign as necessary (Kimbell, 1982); initiation, exploration, concept formulation, preliminary design and development, detailed design and development, modifications, and improvements (Edel, 1967); orientation, corporation, analysis, hypothesis, incubation, synthesis, verification (Osborn, 1953).

Two   The Brief: Begin with the End in Mind

1. Some of the following has been adapted from Bernstein, 1988; Blyth and Worthington, 2001; Boyle, 2004; Bruce and Bessant, 2002; Rugg and Blandford, 1997; Thackara, 1997; as well as the others cited.

Three   Research: The Art of Seeing the Different Way

1. IDEO is a well-known and well-regarded Southern California-based international consultancy that helps companies innovate. According to their website (www.ideo.com) they design products, services, environments, and digital experiences.
2. Adapted from the set of fifty-one IDEO method cards available from www.ideo.com.
3. The move from products to solutions is a form of commoditization where you systematize a process; e.g., if a consultancy turns its change management or technology implementation or cultural analysis processes into a tool or product, it can change its business model or offer "fixed" prices to clients.
4. Adapted from the IDEO method cards available from www.ideo.com.
5. According to Leonard and Straus (1998), "The most widely recognized cognitive distinction is between left-brained and right-brained ways of thinking. This categorization is more powerful metaphorically than it is accurate physiologically; not all the functions commonly associated with the left brain are located on the left side of the cortex and not all so-called right brained functions are located on the right. Still, the simple description does usefully capture radically different ways of thinking" (pp. 112–113).

Five   Prototyping: Making an Idea Clearly Visible

1. Todd is head teacher of interior design at TAFE Sydney Institute's Design Centre, Enmore, one of Australia's leading design colleges. He is passionate about design and creativity, and is a councillor of the New South Wales Design Institute of Australia. Prior to teaching, Todd worked as an interior designer for high-profile corporate design firms in Sydney and Melbourne, Australia.
2. Karen Lewis is assistant professor in the School of Architecture, at the University of Kentucky's College of Design. She specializes in designs that combine architecture and landscape architecture, emphasizing program and community, infrastructure, and memorable place-making. She has a master of architecture degree from Harvard University, Graduate School of Design, Cambridge, MA, and a BA in architecture with honors from Wellesley College, Wellesley, MA.

Seven   Delivery: Output and Presentation

1. Two of those interviewed expressed a different opinion and suggested that presenting one option was their preference: "I always give them my preferred model. I would say I have others but I'd go with one. This is what I have come up with. That is what they are paying me for" (Kay, Interior Designer); "My default is to show 'the one,' however, the client is an essential part of the process and I will present options to involve the client especially at the start. I never present one I am not happy with" (Todd, Interior Designer, Design Educator).

BIBLIOGRAPHY

Altier, W. (1988). From experience: A perspective on creativity. *Journal of Product Innovation Management*, vol. 5, 154–161.

American Planning Association. (2006). *Healthier Neighborhoods* (www.planning.org), March.

Anders, R. (2000). Defining, mapping, and designing the design process. *Design Management Journal*, vol. 1, # 3, no page number available.

Anggreeni, I. & van der Voort, M. (2008). Tracing the scenarios in scenario-based product design: A study to understand scenario generation. *Design Principles and Practices: An International Journal*, vol. 2, # 4, 123–135.

Ante, S. (2006). Ethnographic hits. *Business Week* On-line Magazine (ww.businessweek.com), June 5.

Archer, B. (1979). Design as a discipline. *Design Studies*, vol 1, # 1, 17–20.

Ashkenas, R. and Francis, S. (2000). Integration managers: Special leaders for special times. *Harvard Business Review*, vol. 78, # 6, 108–116.

Badke-Schaub, P. & Frankenberger, E. (1997). Modelling design processes of groups in industry: and empirical investigation of cooperative design work (347–354). In D. Harris (ed.), *Engineering psychology and cognitive ergonomics*, volume two. Ashgate: London.

Baek, S. & Lee, K. (2008). A participatory design approach to information architecture design for children. *CoDesign*, vol. 4, # 3, 173–191.

Ball, L., Ormerod, T., & Maskill, L. (1997). "Satisficing" in engineering design: Psychological determinants and implications for design support (347–354). In Harris, *Engineering psychology and cognitive ergonomics*, volume two.

Barney, J. (1991). Firm resources and sustained competitive advantage. *Journal of Management*, vol. 17, # 1, 99–120.

———. (1999). Looking inside for competitive advantage (128–141). In R. Schuler and S. Jackson (eds.), *Strategic human resource management*. Blackwell: Malden, MA.

———. (2001). Is the resource-based "view" a useful perspective for strategic management research? Yes. *Academy of Management Review*, vol. 26, # 1, 41–56.

Bartlett, J. & Toms, E. (2005). Developing a protocol for bioinformatics analysis: An integrated information behaviour and task analysis approach. *Journal of the American Society for Information Science and Technology*, vol. 56, # 5, 469–482.

Barwise, P. & Meehan, S. (2004). Don't be unique, be better. *MIT Sloan Management Review*, vol. 45, # 4, 23–26.

Baskerville, R. & Stage, J. (1996). Controlling prototype development through risk analysis. *MIS Quarterly*, vol. 20, # 4, 481–503.

Basu, S. (2008). How students design and enact physics lessons: Five immigrant Caribbean youth and the cultivation of student voice. *Journal of Research in Science Teaching*, vol. 45, # 8, 881–899.

Bayus, B. (1995). Optimal dynamic policies for product and process innovation. *Journal of Operations Management*, vol. 12, # 3, 173–185.

Bazeley, P. (2003). Computerized data analysis for mixed methods research (385–422). In A. Tashakkori & C. Teddlie (eds.), *Handbook of mixed methods in social & behavioural research.* Sage: Thousand Oaks, CA.

Beall, D. (2001). Strategy execution. *The Strategy House Inc.*, vol. 2, # 2, 1–2.

Beaver, G. (2001). Strategy, management creativity and corporate history. *Strategic Change*, vol. 10, # 1, 1–4.

Bell, G. (2004a). Insights into Asia: Same technologies, different attitudes and reasons for years. *Technology@Intel* Magazine, May.

———. (2004b). Insights into Asia: Same technologies, different attitudes and reasons for years. *Technology@Intel* Magazine, June.

Berk, J. (2006). Change champions. *The Internal Auditor*, vol. 63, # 2, 64–69.

Bernstein, D. (1988). The design mind (202–216). In Peter Gorb (ed.), *Design talks, London Business School.* London: The Design Council.

Bevan, G. (2006). The industrial design process. In James Tuckerman (ed.), *Industrial design showcase.* Australian Anthill, February–March.

Bilton, C. (2007). *Management and creativity: From creative industries to creative management.* Blackwell: U.K.

Binder, T. & Brandt, E. (2008). The Design Lab as platform in participatory design research. *CoDesign*, vol. 4, # 2, 115–129.

Black, M. (1975). The designer and manager syndrome (41–55). In Schutte (ed.), *The uneasy coalition: Design in corporate America.*

Blyth, A. & Worthington, J. (2001). *Managing the brief for better design.* Taylor & Francis: London.

Blythe, S., Grabill, J., & Riley, K. (2008). Action research and wicked environmental problems. *Journal of Business and Technical Communication*, vol. 22, # 3, 272–298.

Boland, R. & Collopy, F. (2004). *Managing as designing.* Stanford: CA.

Bonabeau, E. & Meyer, C. (2001). Swarm intelligence: A whole new way to think about business. *Harvard Business Review*, vol. 79, # 5, 107–114.

Bordac, S. & Rainwater, J. (2008). User-Centered Design in Practice: The Brown University Experience. *Journal of Web Librarianship*, vol. 2, # 2/3, 109–138.

Borghini, S. (2005). Organizational creativity: breaking equilibrium and order to innovate. *Journal of Knowledge Management*, vol. 9, # 4, 19–33.

Boyle, G. (2004). *Design project management.* Ashgate: London.

Bozionelos, N. (2005). When the inferior candidate is offered the job: The selection interview as a political and power game. *Human Relations*, vol. 58, # 12, 1605–1631.

Brotchie, A. (1995). *A book of surrealist games.* Shambhala: Boston, MA.

Brown, D. (2007). *Communicating design.* Peachpit: Berkeley, CA.

Brown, S. & Eisenhardt, K. (1995). Product development: Past research, present findings, and future directions. *The Academy of Management Review*, vol. 20, # 2, 343–378.

Brown, T. (2005). Strategy by design. *Fast Company*, June, # 95, 52–54.

———. (2008). Design thinking. *Harvard Business Review*, vol. 86, # 6, 84–92.

Bruce, M. (2002). Creating design futures (255–277). In Bruce and Bessant, *Design in Business.*

Bruce, A., Lampel, J., & Mintzberg, H. (1999). Strategy, blind men and the elephant. *Financial Times*, September 27, 6.

Bruce, M. & Bessant, J. (Eds) (2002). *Design in business*. Harlow: London.

Bundy, W. (2002). *Innovation, creativity, and discovery in modern organisations*. Quorum: Westport, CT.

Burian, R. (2005). The critical role of creativity. *BusinessWeek*, August 22, # 3948, 18.

Buzan, T. (2000). *The mind map book*. BBC: London.

———. (2004). *Mind maps at work*. Thorsons: London.

Cagliano, R., Acur, N., & Boer, H. (2005). Patterns of change in manufacturing strategy configurations. *International Journal of Operations & Production Management*, vol. 25, # 7, 701–718.

Cameron, K. & Quinn, R. (1999). *Diagnosing and changing organizational culture*. Addison-Wesley: Reading, MA.

Camillus, J. (2008). Strategy as a wicked problem. *Harvard Business Review*, vol. 86, # 5, 98–106.

Cao, G., Clarke, S., & Lehaney, B. (2001). A critique of BPR from a holistic perspective. *Business Process Management Journal*, vol. 7, # 4, 332–339.

Carlopio, J. (1994). Holism: A philosophy of organisational leadership for the future. *The Leadership Quarterly*, # 3/4, 297–307.

———. (1996a). Holistic organisational health: Curing the part by focusing on the whole (1–20). In A. Gutschelhofer & J. Scheff (eds), *Paradoxical management*. Linde: Austria.

———. (1996b). Construct validity of a physical work environment satisfaction questionnaire. *Journal of Occupational Health Psychology*, vol 1, 330–344.

———. (1998). *Implementation: Making workplace innovation and technical change happen*. McGraw-Hill: Sydney.

———. (2003). *Changing gears: The strategic implementation of new technology*. Palgrave Macmillan: London.

Carlopio, J. & Gardner, D. (1992). Direct and interactive effects of the physical work environment on attitudes. *Environment and Behavior*, vol. 24, 579–601.

Carney, M. (2004a). Perceptions of professional clinicians and non-clinicians on their involvement in strategic planning in health care management: Implications for interdisciplinary involvement. *Nursing and Health Sciences*, vol. 6, 321–328.

———. (2004b). Middle manager involvement in strategy development in not-for-profit organizations: The director of nursing perspective—how organizational structure impacts on the role. *Journal of Nursing Management*, vol. 12, 13–21.

———. (2007). How commitment and involvement influence the development of strategic consensus in healthcare organizations: The multidisciplinary approach. *Journal of Nursing Management*, vol. 15, 649–658.

Carr, A. & Pearson, J. (2002). The impact of purchasing and supplier involvement on strategic purchasing and its impact on firm's performance. *International Journal of Operations & Production Management*, vol. 22, # 9/10, 1032–1054.

Carroll, J. (1995). *Scenario-based design: Envisioning work and technology in system development*. Wiley: New York.

Carson, D., Gilmore, A., Perry, C., & Gronhaug, K. (2001). *Qualitative marketing research*. Sage: London.

Catenazzo, G. & Fragniere, E. (2009). Do travel agencies provide sufficient value to their clients? Paper presented at the 4th International Conference on Services Management, Oxford Brookes University, May 8–9.

Ceylan, C., Dul, J., & Aytac, S. (2008). Can the office environment stimulate a manager's creativity? ERIM Report Series Reference No. ERS-2008–059-LIS. Available at SSRN: http://ssrn.com/abstract=1268579

Chakraborty, K. (1997). Sustained competitive advantage: A resource-based framework. *Advances in Competitiveness Research*, vol. 5, # 1, 32–63.

Chamorro-Koc, M. (2008). *Useability, experience and context-of-use.* VDM Verlag: Saarbrucken, Germany.

Chhatpar, R. (2007). Innovate faster by melding design and strategy. *Harvard Business Review,* vol. 85, # 9, 30–32.

Christensen, K. (2009). Building shared understanding of wicked problems. *Rotman Magazine,* Winter, 16–20.

Clark, K., Smith, R., & Yamazaki, K. (2006). Experience design that drives consideration. *Design Management Review,* vol. 17, # 1, 47–56.

Clarke, M., Butcher, D., & Bailey, C. (2004). Strategically aligned leadership development (271–291). In J. Story (ed.), *Leadership in organizations.* Routledge: London.

Clegg, B. (1999). *Creativity and innovation for managers.* Butterworth-Heinemann: Oxford.

Cohen, L. (1988). Quality function deployment. *National Productivity Review,* vol. 7, # 3, 197–208.

Collier, N., Fishwick, F., & Floyd, S. (2004). Managerial involvement and perceptions of strategy process. *Long Range Planning,* vol. 3, # 1, 67–83.

Conklin, J. (2006). *The dialogue mapping: building shared understanding of wicked problems.* Wiley: West Sussex, England.

Coughlan, P. & Prokopoff, I (2006). Managing change, by design. *Rotman Magazine,* Winter, 20–23.

Coutu, D (2002). Spotting patterns on the fly. *Harvard Business Review,* vol. 80, # 11, 45–49.

Cravens, D. (1998). Examining the impact of market-based strategy paradigms on marketing strategy. *Journal of Strategic Marketing,* vol. 6, 197–208.

Crewe, K. (2001). The quality of participatory design: The effects of citizen input on the design of the Boston Southwest corridor. *Journal of the American Planning Association,* vol. 67, # 4, 437–455.

Cross, N. (1982). Designerly ways of knowing. *Design Studies,* vol. 3, # 4, 221–226.

———. (2000). *Engineering design methods.* Wiley: Chichester.

Cross, N., Dorst, K., & Roozenburg, N. (1992). *Research in design thinking.* Delft University Press: Delft.

Daniell, M. (2004). *Strategy: A step-by-step approach to the development and presentation of world class business strategy.* Palgrave McMillan: Hampshire, U.K.

Davies, R. (2004). Adapting virtual reality for the participatory design of work environments. *Computer Supported Cooperative Work,* vol. 13, 1–33.

Davis, D., Ringsted, C., Bonde, M., Scherpbier, A., & van der Vleuten, C. (2009). Using participatory design to develop structured training in child and adolescent psychiatry. *European Child & Adolescent Psychiatry,* vol. 18, # 1, 33–41.

Davis, M., Hawley, P., McMullan, B., & Spilka, G. (1997). *Design as a catalyst for learning.* Association for Supervision and Curriculum Development: Alexandria, Virginia.

Day, L. (1893). Of designs and working drawings. *Arts and Crafts Essays* (accessed via chestofbooks.com, March 17, 2009).

deBono, E. (1969). Information processing and new ideas—lateral and critical thinking. *Value Engineering,* vol. 1, # 5, 195–200.

———. (1985). *Six thinking hats.* Little, Brown & Co.: Boston, MA.

Deluzio, M. & Hawkey, B. (2006). Strategy deployment: Effective alignment of LEAN to drive profitability growth. *Cost Management,* vol. 20, # 2, 30–39.

Design Council UK. (February 26, 2006) www.design-council.org.uk.

DiDio, L. (2005). Warring vendors give peace a chance. *CIO Today,* www.cio-today.com, November 11.

Ditkoff, M. (1998). Ten skills for brainstorming: Breakthrough thinking. *The Journal for Quality and Participation,* vol. 21, # 6, 30–32.

Dodgson, M., Gann, D., & Salter, A. (2005). *Think, play, do.* Oxford University Press: Oxford, U.K.

Donaldson, L. (1985). *In defence of organizational theory.* Cambridge University Press: Cambridge.

———. (1991). *The contingency theory of organizations.* Sage: CA.

Dowding, T. & Johnson, R. (2008). How many users does it really take?: Revising usability testing. *Design Principles and Practices: An International Journal,* vol. 2, # 2, 65–72.

Drew, S. (2006). Building technology foresight: Using scenarios to embrace innovation. *European Journal of Innovation Management,* vol. 9, # 3, 241.

Drew, S. & West, D. (2002). Design and competitive advantage: Strategies for market acceptance. *Journal of General Management,* vol. 28, # 2, 58–72.

Drewniany, B. & Jewler, A. (2008). *Creative strategy in advertising.* Thomson: Boston, MA.

Dreyfuss, H. (1955/2003). *Designing for people.* 1955 edition published by Simon and Schuster. 2003 edition published by Allworth: New York.

Dunne, P. & Young, S. (2004). Thinking beyond 4,000 pounds of metal. *Executive Agenda,* vol. 7, # 4, 25–31.

Durant, R., Legge, J. (2006). "Wicked problems," public policy, and administrative theory. *Administration and Society,* vol. 38, # 3, 309–334.

Dutson, A. & Wood, K. (2005). Using rapid prototypes for functional evaluation of evolutionary product designs. *Rapid Prototyping Journal,* vol. 11, # 3, 125–131.

Eason, K. (1997). Inventing the future: Collaborative design of socio-technical systems (3–10). In Harris, *Engineering psychology and cognitive ergonomics,* volume two.

Edel, D. (1967). *Introduction to creative design.* Prentice-Hall: New Jersey.

Eden, C. & Ackerman, F. (1998). *Making strategy: The journey of strategic management.* Sage: London.

Eisenhardt, K. & Sull, D. (2001). Strategy as simple rules. *Harvard Business Review,* vol. 79, # 1, 107–116.

Elias, M. (2004). Sunlight reduces need for pain medication. *USA Today,* March 3.

Ellingson, M. (1933). Education and research at a mechanics institute: III. Activity analysis. *Personnel Journal,* vol. 12, 12–15.

Emmitt, S. (2002). *Architectural technology.* Blackwell Science: Oxford, U.K.

Endsley, M., Bolte, B., & Jones, D. (2003). *Designing for situational awareness.* Taylor & Francis: London.

Erickson, T. (1995). Notes on design practice: Stories and prototypes as catalysts for communication (37–58). In Carroll, *Scenario-based design: Envisioning work and technology in system development.*

Eunni, R., Kasuganti, R., & Kos, A. (2006). Knowledge management processes in international business alliances: a review. *International Journal of Management,* vol. 23, # 1, 34–42.

Evans, J. (1991). *Creative thinking in the decision and management sciences.* South-Western Publishing Company: Cincinnati, Ohio.

Evans, M. & Campbell, R. (2003). A comparative evaluation of industrial design models produced using rapid prototyping. *Rapid Prototyping Journal,* vol 9, # 5, 344–351.

Farnham, D. & Horton, S. (2003). Organisational change and staff participation and involvement in Britain's public services. *The International Journal of Public Sector Management,* vol. 16, # 6, 434–448.

Florida, R. (2002). *The rise of the creative class.* Basic Books: New York.

Fluharty, B. (2004). A place at the table: Taking design from service to corporate functions. *Design Management Review,* vol. 15, # 2, 17–24.

Formosa, K. & Kroeter, S. (2002). Toward design literacy in American management: A strategy for MBA programs. *Design Management Journal,* vol. 13, # 3, 46–54.

Francis, D. (2002). Strategy and design (61–75). In M. Bruce and J. Bessant (eds.), *Design in business*. Harlow: London.

Fraser, H. (2007). The practice of breakthrough strategies by design. *Journal of Business Strategy*, vol. 28, # 4, 66–74.

Freeman, K. (2005). Making acquisitions work. *Strategy+business*, Fall, # 40, 1–3.

Friedman, K. (2002). Towards an integrative design discipline. In S. Squires and B. Byrne (Eds.), *Creating Breakthrough Ideas: The Collaboration of Anthropologists and Designers in the Product Development* Industry. Bergin & Gravey: London.

Fulton Suri, J. (2005). *Thoughtless acts? Observations on intuitive design*. Chronicle: San Francisco.

Gadiesh, O. & Gilbert, J. L. (2001). Transforming corner-office strategy into frontline action. *Harvard Business Review*, May, vol. 79, # 5, 73–79.

Gibb, S. & Waight, C. (2005). Connecting HRD and creativity: From fragmentary insights to strategic significance. *Advances in Developing Human Resources*, vol. 7, # 2, 271–286.

Gierke, M., Hanson, J., and Turner, R. (2002). Wise counsel: A trinity of perspectives on the business value of design. *Journal Boston*, vol. 13, # 1, 10–17.

Godin, S. (2001). *Purple cow*. Penguin: London, UK.

———. (2005). *The big moo: Stop trying to be perfect and start being remarkable*. Penguin: New York.

Goldsby-Smith, T. (2007). The second road of thought: how design offers strategy a new toolkit. *Journal of Business Strategy*, vol. 28, # 4, 22–29.

Goldsmith, R., d'Hauteville, F., & Flynn, L. (1998). Theory and measurement of consumer innovativeness: A transnational evaluation. *European Journal of Marketing*, vol. 32, # 3/4, 340–353.

Gorb, P. (1990). Design management. Papers from the London business School, architecture design and technology press. London, U.K.

———. (1990). The future of design and its management (15–25). In M. Oakley (ed.), *Design management: A handbook of issues and methods*. Blackwell: Cambridge, MA.

Grant, D. (2006, March). Personal communications.

Green, M. (2007). Emotions across media: Transportation into written and filmed narratives. Conference Papers—International Communication Association, 2007 Annual Meeting, p. 1.

———. (2008). Research challenges in narrative persuasion. *Information Design Journal*, vol. 16, # 1, 47–52.

Green, M. & Brock, T. (2000). The role of transportation in the persuasiveness of public narratives. *Journal of Personality & Social Psychology*, vol. 79, # 5, 701–721.

Green, M., Brock, T. & Kaufman, G. (2004). Understanding media enjoyment: The role of transportation into narrative worlds. *Communication Theory*, vol. 14, # 4, 311–327.

Green, M., Kass, S., Carrey, J., Herzig, B., Feeney, R., & Sabini, J. (2008). Transportation across media: Repeated exposure to print and film. *Media Psychology*, vol. 11, # 4, 512–539.

Grint, K. (2005). Problems, problems, problems: The social construction of "leadership." *Human Relations*, vol. 58, # 11, 1467–1494.

Gummesson, E. (2000). *Qualitative methods in management research*. Sage: CA.

Hadfield, P. (2003). Ecowar looms in the Pacific's pristine waters. *New Scientist*, 22 February, # 2383.

Hambrick, D. & Fredrickson, J. (2005). Are you sure you have a strategy? *The Academy of the Management Executive*, vol. 19, # 4, sp 51.

Hamel, G. (1997). Killer strategies that make stakeholders rich. *Fortune*, vol. 135, # 12, 70.

———. (1998). Strategy emergence. *Executive Excellence*, vol. 15, # 12, 3–4.

Hamel, G. & Prahalad, C. (1995). Seeing the future first. *Executive Excellence*, vol. 12, # 11, 15–16.

Haskell, D. (1940). The world of design. *Nation*, vol. 150, # 15, 489–490.

Hattersley, M. (1997). The managerial art of telling a story. *Harvard Management Update*, January, 3–4.

Haweis, H. (1878). *The art of beauty*. Chatto & Windus: London.

Hearn, L. (2006). Australian banks "fail" in online mission. *Sydney Morning Herald*, July 25.

Henderson, B. (1979). *Henderson on corporate strategy*. Mentor: New York.

Hock, D. (1999). *Birth of the chaordic age*. Berrett-Koehler: San Francisco, CA.

Hodgkinson, M. (2002). A shared strategic vision: Dream or reality? *The Learning Organization*, vol. 9, # 2, 89–95.

Holt, K. (1990). The nature of the design process (195–205). In Oakley, *Design management*.

Hoving, W. (1975). Foreword (ix–x). In Schutte, *The uneasy coalition: Design in corporate America*.

Hsu, K. (2005). Using balanced scorecard and fuzzy data envelopment analysis for multinational R & D project performance assessment. *Journal of American Academy of Business*, vol. 7, # 1, 189–196.

Hughes, G. (2003). Add creativity to your decision processes. *The Journal for Quality & Participation*, Summer, 5–13.

Hunter, D. (2006). Leadership resilience and tolerance for ambiguity in crisis situations. *The Business Review*, vol. 5, # 1, 44–50.

Institute of Directors. (2002). *Directors on design*. Director Publications: London, U.K.

Jeyaraj, A. Rottman, J., & Lacity, M. (2006). A review of the predictors, linkages, and biases in IT innovation adoption research. *Journal of Information Technology*, vol. 21, 1–23.

Jirotka, M. & Luff, P. (2006). Supporting requirements with video-based analysis. *IEEE Software*, May/June, 42–44.

Johnson, B. & Turner, L. (2003). Data collection strategies in mixed methods research (297–319). In Tashakkori & Teddlie, *Handbook of mixed methods in social & behavioural research*.

Johnson, D., Donohue, W., Atkin, C., & Johnson, S. (2001). Communication, involvement, and perceived innovativeness: Tests of a model with two contrasting innovations. *Group & Organization Management*, vol. 26, # 1, 24–52.

Johnson, P., Johnson, H., & Wilson, S. (1995). Rapid prototyping of user interfaces driven by task models (209–246). In Carroll, *Scenario-based design: Envisioning work and technology in system development*.

Johnston, R. & Bate, J. (2003). *The power of strategy innovation*. AMACOM: New York.

Jonk, J. & Ungerath, M. (2006). Mergers and acquisitions: Not so fast—Companies need to pace themselves during the integration process. *Financier Worldwide*, January.

Joyce, A. (2008). Crowdsourcing creativity: participant in design on the Internet. *Design Principles and Practices: An International Journal*, vol. 1, # 3, 87–93.

Jung, P. & Cherng, E. (2005). It's crunch time. What's ahead for tech and telecom? *Executive Agenda*, vol. 8, # 2, 23–33.

Kahneman, D. & Tversky, A. (1979a). Prospect theory: An analysis of decisions under risk. *Econometrica*, vol. 47, 313–327.

McFall, B. & Beacham, C. (2008). Delimiting wicked problems to initiate design solutions. Design 08: The second international conference on design principles and practices, University of Miami, January 9–11.

Makridakis & S. C. Wheelwright (eds), *Studies in the management sciences: Forecasting*. Amsterdam: North Holland.

Kazui, H., Mori, E., Hashimoto, M., & Hiro, H. (2003). Enhancement of declarative memory by emotional arousal and visual memory function in Alzheimer's disease. *The Journal of Neuropsychiatry and Clinical Neurosciences*, vol. 15, # 2, 221–226.

Kane, K. (2007). Anthropologists go native in the corporate village. www.fastcompany.com.

Kelley, T. (2005). *The ten faces of innovation.* Doubleday: New York.

Kim, S. (1990). *Essence of creativity.* Oxford University Press: Oxford, U.K.

Kim, W. & Mauborgne, R. (1999). Creating new market space. *Harvard Business Review,* January–February, 83–93.

Kim, W. & Mauborgne, R. (2004). Blue Ocean strategy. *Harvard Business Review,* October, 76–84.

Kimbell, R. (1982). *Design education.* Routledge: London, U.K.

Kimbell, R., Stables, K., & Green, R. (1996). *Understanding practice in design and technology.* Open University Press: Buckingham, U.K.

Kimbell, R., Stables, K., Wheeler, T., Wozniak, A., & Kelly, V. (1991). *The assessment of performance in design and technology.* School Examinations and Assessment Council: London, U.K.

Kneeshaw, D. (2005). Personal communications.

———. (2006). *Creative strategic thinking executive program materials.* Australian Graduate School of Management: University of New South Wales, Sydney Australia.

Kreuter, M., De Rosa, C., Howze, E., & Baldwin, G. (2004). Understanding wicked problems: A key to advancing environmental health promotion. *Health Education and Behavior,* vol. 31, # 4, 441–454.

Laabs, J. (2003). Corporate anthropologists (29–34). In A. Podolefsky & P. Brown (eds.), Applying cultural anthropology. McGraw-Hill: Boston, MA.

Lajocono, G. & Zaccai, G. (2004). The evolution of the design-inspired enterprise. *MIT Sloan Management Review,* Spring, 75–79.

Lauer, D. & Pentak, S. (2008). *Design basics.* Thomson: Boston, MA.

Lawson, B. (2004). *What designers know.* Elsevier: Oxford, U.K.

———. (2006). *How designers think: The design process demystified* (fourth edition). Elsevier: Oxford, UK.

Lebihan, R. (2004). IT screw-ups take a toll on mergers. *Australian Financial Review,* January 8.

Le Theule, M. & Fronda, Y (2005). The organization in tension between creation and rationalization: facing management views to artistic and scientific creators. *Critical Perspectives on Accounting,* vol. 16, 749–786.

Leonard, D. & Straus, S. (1998). Putting your company's whole brain to work (109–136). In *The Harvard Business Review on Knowledge Management.* Harvard College: Boston, MA.

Lester, R, Piore, M., & Malek, K. (1998). Interpretive management: What general managers can learn from design. *Harvard Business Review,* vol. 76, # 2, 86–96.

Liedtka, J. (2000). In defense of strategy as design. *California Management Review,* vol. 42, # 3, 8–23.

Liedtka, J. & Rosenblum, J. (1996). Shaping conversations: Making strategy, managing change. *California Management Review,* vol. 39, # 1, 141–157.

Liem, A. (2005). Introducing form and user sensivity to mechanical engineering students through industrial design projects (269–274). In P. Rogers, L. Brohurst, & D. Hepburn (eds.), *Crossing design boundaries.* Taylor & Francis: London, U.K.

Light, A., Blythe, M., & Reed, D. (2007). Defamiliarising design. *Design Principles and Practices: An International Journal,* vol. 1, # 4, 63–72.

Lim, C., Winter, R., & Chan, C. (2006). Cross-cultural interviewing in the hiring process: challenges and strategies. *The Career Development Quarterly,* vol. 54, # 3, 265–268.

Lockwood, T. (2004). Integrating design into organizational culture. *Design Management Review,* vol. 15, # 2, 32–39.

Lovallo, D., & Kahneman, D. (2003). Delusions of success: How optimism undermines executives' decisions. *Harvard Business Review,* vol. 81, # 7, 56–63.

Lyles, M. (1987). Defining strategic problems: Subjective criteria of executives. *Organization Studies*, vol 8, # 3, 263–280.

Lynch, J. (1982). On the external validity of experiments in consumer research. *Journal of Consumer Research*, vol. 9, # 3, 225–239.

Macaulay, C., Sloan, D., Jiang, X., Forbes, P., Loynton, S., Swedlow, J., and Gregor, P. (2009). Usability and user-centered design in scientific software development. *IEEE Software*, vol. 1, 96–102.

Machever, W. (1962). Is the hard line here to stay? *Management of Personnel Quarterly*, vol. 1, # 2, 24–29.

MacLean, A. & McKerlie, D. (1995). Design space analysis and use representations (183–207). In Carroll, *Scenario-based design: Envisioning work and technology in system development*.

Mair, G., Miller, K., and Anderson, A. (2005). Multimodel design imaging—A vehicle for crossing design boundaries (27–32). In Rogers, Brohurst, & Hepburn, *Crossing design boundaries*.

Manzari, L. & Trinidad-Christensen, J. (2006). User-centered design of a web site for library and information science students: heuristic evaluation and usability testing. *Information Technology and Libraries*, vol. 25, # 3, 163–169.

March, L. (1976). The Logic of Design. In L. March (ed.), *The Architecture of Form*. Cambridge University Press: Cambridge, U.K.

March, J. & Simon, H. (1958). *Organizations*. New York: Wiley.

Marsh, P. (2001). White goods with a fresh spin. *Financial Times*, June 19, 20.

Martin, R. (2005a). Creativity that goes deep. *BusinessWeek* Online August 3.

———. (2005b). Why decisions need design. *BusinessWeek* Online, August 30.

———. (2005c). Reliability vs. Validity. *BusinessWeek* Online, September 29.

Martinez, R. & Artiz, K. (2006). An examination of firm slack and risk-taking in regulated and deregulated airlines. *Journal of Management Issues*, vol. 18, # 1, 11–32.

McClelland, D. (1976). *The achieving society*. Irvington: New York.

———. (1985). *Human motivation*. Scott, Foresman: New York.

McCullagh, K. (2006). Strategy for the real world. *Design Management Review*, Fall, 48–55.

McGahan, A. (2004). How industries change. *Harvard Business Review*, October, 87–94.

McGrath, K. (2006, March). Personal communication.

McGregor, J. (2006). The world's most innovative companies. *Business Week*, April 24, # 3981, 62.

McKee, R. (2003). Storytelling that moves people. *Harvard Business Review*, vol. 81, # 6, 51–55.

McKenna, T. (2002). Strategy development and the human component. *National Petroleum News*, March, 20.

Meagher, D. (2006). Wild at heart. *The AFR magazine*, April, 58–63.

Michlewski, K. (2008). Uncovering design attitude: Inside the culture of designers. *Organization Studies*, vol. 29, # 3, 373–392.

Miles, R. & Snow, C. (1984). Designing strategic human resources systems. *Organizational Dynamics*, vol 13, # 1, 36–52.

Mintzberg, H. (1990). The design school: Reconsidering the basic premises of strategic management. *Strategic Management Journal*, vol. 11, # 3, 171–195.

Mintzberg, H. & Lampel, J. (1999). Reflecting on the strategy process. *MIT Sloan Management Review*, vol. 40, # 3, 21–30.

Mintzberg, H. & Waters, J. (1985). Of strategies, deliberate and emergent. *Strategic Management Journal*, vol. 6, # 3, 257–273.

Mintzberg, H., Ahlstrand, B., & Lampel, J. (1998). *Strategy safari*. Free Press: New York.

Mitchell, L. (2005). Design key to innovation economy. *The Age* (www.theage.com.au), July 11.

Mockler, R. (2006). Integratively balancing structured and unstructured thinking in business management. *The Business Review*, vol. 5, # 1, 1–7.

Morecroft, J. (1984). Strategy support models. *Strategic Management Journal*, vol. 5, # 3, 215–229.

———. (1992). Executive knowledge, models and learning. *European Journal of Operations Research*, vol. 59, # 1, 9–27.

———. (1999). Management attitudes, learning and scale in successful diversification: A dynamic and behavioural resource systems view. *Journal of Operational Research Society*, vol. 50, 215–229.

Morecroft, J. & Sterman, J. (1994). *Modeling for learning organizations*. Productivity Press: Portland, OR.

Moughtin, C., Cuesta, R., Sarris, C., & Signoretta, P. (2003). *Urban design: Method and techniques*. Architectural Press: Oxford, U.K.

Mukherji, A. & Mukherji, J. (2003). Understanding strategy: Why is strategy so difficult? *Advances in Competitiveness Research*, vol. 11, # 1, 1–19.

Myers, K. & Briggs, I. (1998). *Introduction to type (6th ed.)*. Consulting Psychologists Press: Palo Alto, CA.

Nadler, G. (1980). A timeline theory of planning and design. *Design Studies*, vol. 1, # 5, 299–307.

Neals, S. (2006). Fuel solution: Out of the box. *CSIRO Solve*, # 9, November, p. 11.

Norman, D. (2004). *Emotional design*. Basic: New York.

Nussbaum, B. (2004). The power of design. *BusinessWeek* Online (www.businessweek.com), May 17.

———. (2006). Ethnography is the new core competence. *BusinessWeek* Online (www.businessweek.com), June 16.

Oakley, M. (1984). *Managing product design*. Weidenfeld and Nicolson: London.

———. (1990). Design and design management (1–14). In Oakley, *Design management*.

Oosthuizen, H. (2000). Developing strategy—do we really need a new paradigm? *South African Journal of Business Management*, vol. 31, # 1, 9–14.

Ormerod, T., Rummer, R., & Ball, L. (1999). An ecologically valid study of categorisation by designers (471–478). In Harris, *Engineering psychology and cognitive ergonomics*, volume four.

Osborn, A. (1953). *Applied imagination*. Scribner: New York.

Page, J. (1963). Review of the papers presented at the conference. J. Jones and D. Thornley (eds.), *Conference on Design Methods*. Pergamon: Oxford, U.K.

Papanek, V. (1971). *Design for the real world: Human ecology and social change*. Pantheon Books: New York.

———. (1984). *Design for the real world: Human ecology and social change*, 2nd edition. Thames and Hudson: London.

Papert, S. (1980). *Mindstorms: Children, computers, and powerful ideas*. New York: Basic Books.

Park, J. (2008). A model of experience test for web designers. *Design Principles and Practices: An International Journal*, vol. 2, # 1, 175–182.

Peters, T. (2005). *Design*. DK: New York.

Pilditch, J. (1990). Using design effectively (13–23). In P. Gorb (ed.), *Design management*. Architecture Design and Technology Press: London.

Pink, D. (2003). How does Ideo come up with one-hit innovation after another? *Fast Company*, vol. 75, 104–105.

Pitt, M. & Clarke, K. (1999). Competing on competence: A knowledge perspective on the management of strategic innovation. *Technology Analysis & Strategic Management*, vol. 11, # 3, 301–316.

Plach, M., Wallach, D., & Wintermantel, M. (1999). Supporting the anticipation-feedback loop in user interface design (395–401). In Harris, *Engineering psychology and cognitive ergonomics*, volume four.

Polster, B., Neumann, C., Schuler, M., & Leven, F. (2004). *A-Z of modern design*. Merrell: New York.

Porter, M. (1980). *Competitive strategy*. Free Press: New York.

———. (1996). What is strategy? *Harvard Business Review*, vol. 74, # 6, 61–78.

Postrel, V. (2003). *The substance of style*. Harper: New York.

Prahalad, C. (1993). The role of core competencies in the corporation. *Research Technology Management*, vol. 36, # 6, 40–47.

———. (2005). *The fortune at the bottom of the pyramid*. Pearson: NJ.

Prahalad, C. & Hamel, G. (1990). The core competence of the corporation. *Harvard Business Review*, vol. 68, # 3, 79–91.

Press, M. & Cooper, R. (2003). *The design experience*. Ashgate: Aldershot, U.K.

Pressman, R. (1982). *Software engineering*. McGraw-Hill: New York.

Price, R. (2005). *The eye for innovation*. Yale University: New Haven, CT.

Prichard, J. & Stanton, N. (1999). Testing Belbin's team role theory of effective group functioning (61–68). In Harris, *Engineering psychology and cognitive ergonomics*, volume four.

Quinn, J. B. (1989). Strategic change: "Logical incrementalism." *MIT Sloan Management Review*, Summer, 45–60.

Rainey, D. (2005). *Product innovation*. Cambridge University Press: Cambridge, U.K.

Raps, A. (2004). Implementing strategy. *Strategic Finance*, vol. 85, # 12, 48–53.

Reese, W. (2004). Ethnography for business: Optimizing the impact of industrial design. *Design Management Review*, vol. 15, # 2, 53–59.

Reynolds, P. & Yetton, P. (2006). *Commonwealth securities limited*. Australian Graduate School of Management: Sydney, Australia.

Rice, G. (1977). Structural limits on organizational development. *Human Resource Management*, vol. 16, # 4, 9–13.

Rickards, T. (1992). Creativity and design: Partners in excellence. *Design Management Journal*, vol. 3, # 4, 66–70.

Riis, J., Dukovska-Popovska, I., & Johansen, J. (2006). Participation and dialogue in strategic and you fracturing development. *Production Planning & Control*, vol. 17, # 2, 176–188.

Riley, S. (1998). *Critical thinking and problem solving*. Prentice Hall: Upper Saddle River, NJ.

Rittel, H. & Webber, M. (1973). The dilemmas in a general theory of planning. *Policy Sciences*, vol. 4, # 2, 155–169.

Rizova, P. (2006). Are you networked for successful innovation? *MIT Sloan Management Review*, vol. 47, # 3, 49–55.

Robins, R. (1960). Brainstorming re-evaluated. *Journal of Communication*, vol. 10, # 3, 147–152.

Rogers, E. (1995). *Diffusion of innovations*. Free Press: New York.

Rosson, M. & Carroll, J. (1995). Narrowing the specification-implementation in scenario-based design (247–278). In Carroll, *Scenario-based design: Envisioning work and technology in system development*.

Rubinstein, R. & Hersh, H. (1984). *The human factor*. Digital Press: Bedford, MA.

Rugg, G. & Blandford, A. (1997). Integrating requirements acquisition and user modelling (323–329). In Harris, *Engineering psychology and cognitive ergonomics*, volume two.

Rughase, O. (2006). *Identity and strategy*. Elgar: Cheltenham, U.K.

Ruskin, J. (1837/1838). The poetry of architecture (accessed via www.gutenberg.org, March 17, 2009).

Russo, F. (2006). The hidden secrets of the creative mind. *Time*, vol. 167, # 3, 89–90.

Satran, A. & Kristof, R. (1995). *Interactivity by design*. Adobe Press: CA.

Sauber, T. (2006). *Structured creativity: Formulating an innovation strategy.* Palgrave Macmillan: U.K.

Sawyer, R. (2006). The hidden secrets of the creative mind. *Time,* vol. 167, # 3, 89–90.

Schiffer, M. (2004). The electric vehicle: Technology and expectations in the automobile age. *Business History Review,* vol. 78, # 3, 548–551.

Schoemaker, P. & Gunther, R. (2006). The Wisdom of Deliberate Mistakes. *Harvard Business Review,* vol. 84, # 6, 108–115.

Schrage, M. (2000). *Serious play.* Harvard Business School Press: Boston, MA.

Schultz, G. (2004). Conveyor safety: Task analysis procedure helps identify, reduce risks. *Professional Safety,* vol. 49, # 8, 24–27.

Schutte, T. (1975). *The uneasy coalition: Design in corporate America.* University of Pennsylvania Press: Philadelphia, PA.

Seidel, V. & Pinto, J. (2005). Social science strategies for user-focused innovation and design management. *Design Management Review,* vol. 16, # 4, 73–81.

Seldes, G. (1932). Industrial design, *Saturday Evening Post,* vol. 204, # 48, 34–36.

Sero, M., Guerrero, D., & Munoz, R. (2005). Generating technological knowledge in Spanish universities: An exploration of patent data. *Innovation: Management, Policy & Practice,* vol 7, # 4, 357–372.

Simon, H. (1981). *The sciences of the artificial,* 2nd edition. MIT Press: Cambridge, MA.

Simons, R. (2005). *Levers of organization design.* Harvard Business School Press: Boston, MA.

Slywotzky, A. & Morrison, D. (2000). Pattern thinking: a strategic shortcut. *Strategy & Leadership,* vol. 28, # 1, sp. 12.

Slywotzky, A. & Wise, R. (2003). Double-digit growth in no-growth times. *Fast Company,* # 69, 66–71.

Sowrey, T. (1987). *The generation of ideas for new products.* Kogan Page: London.

Steiner, J. (2005). The art of space management: Planning flexible workspaces for people. *Journal of Facilities Management,* vol. 4, # 1, 6–22.

Sterman, J. (1989). Modeling managerial behavior: Misperceptions of feedback in a dynamic decision making experiment. *Management Science,* vol. 35, # 3, 321–339.

Sterman, J. & Sweeney, L. (2002). Cloudy skies: Assessing public understanding of global warming. *System Dynamics Review,* vol. 18, # 2, 207–214.

Stevens, J., Moultrie, J., & Crilly, N. (2008). How is design strategic? Clarifying the concept of strategic design. *Design Principles and Practices: An International Journal,* vol. 2, # 3, 51–59.

Stiles, E. (2006). *Computer simulations may help CEOs and production managers divine the future.* February 7, 2006, ali.opi Arizona.edu.

Summers, A. (2002). Immaculate conceptions. *Financial Management,* June, sp 20.

Surowiecki, J. (2004). *The wisdom of crowds: Why the many are smarter than the few.* Abacus: London, U.K.

Sutton, R. (2004). The weird rules of creativity (267–275). In M. Tushman and P. Anderson (eds.), *Managing strategic innovation and change.* New York: Oxford University Press.

Swap, W., Leonard, D., Shields, M., & Abrams, L. (2001). Using mentoring and storytelling to transfer knowledge in the workplace. *Journal of Management Information Systems,* vol. 18, # 1, 95–114.

Tai, D. & Huang, C. (2007). The relationship between electronic business process reengineering and organizational performance in Taiwan. *Journal of Academy of Business,* vol. 10, # 2, 296–301.

Tashakkori, A. & Teddlie, C. (2003). *Handbook of mixed methods in social & behavioural research.* Sage: Thousand Oaks, CA.

Taylor, D. (1969). Creative design through functional visualization. *Journal of Creative Behavior,* vol. 3, # 2, 212–214.

Thackara, J. (1997). *Winners! How today's successful companies innovate by design.* Gower: U.K.

Tornatzky, L. & Klein, K. (1982). *Innovation characteristics and innovation adoption-implementation: A meta-analysis of findings.* Washington D.C., National Science Foundation, Division of Industrial Science and Technological Innovation.

Towle, H. (1946). Economic maturity: An industrial view. *The Journal of Business of the University of Chicago,* vol 19, # 4, 224–231.

Turner, D. & Crawford, M. (1998). *Change power.* Business & Professional: Warriewood, Australia.

Ulrich, K. & Eppinger, S. (2004). *Product design and development.* McGraw-Hill: Boston, MA.

van der Heijden, K. (2005). *Scenarios: the art of strategic conversation,* 2nd edition. Wiley: U.K.

van Gaalen, A. (2005). Design: Extreme engineering. *Cosmos,* # 5.

Vaughan, L., Viller, S., Simpson, M., Akama, Y., Yuille, J., & Cooper, R. (2007). Design plus people: An approach to interaction design projects. *Design Principles and Practices: An International Journal,* vol. 1, # 4, 31–36.

Vedin, B. (2005). Future innovation through design (293–303). In C. Wagner (ed.), *Foresight, innovation, and strategy.* World Future Society: Bethesda, Maryland.

Verweire, K. & Berghe, L. (2004). *Integrated performance management: A guide to strategy implementation.* Sage: CA.

Vithayathawornwong, S., Danko, S., & Tolbert, P. (2008). The role of the physical environment in supporting organizational creativity. *Journal of Interior Design,* vol. 29, # 1–2, 1–16.

Vogel, C., Cagan, J., & Boatwright, P. (2005). *The design of things to come.* Pearson Education: New Jersey, U.S.

Wagner, E. & Hansen, E. (2004). A method identifying and assessing key customer group needs. *Industrial Marketing Management,* vol. 33, 643–655.

Wake, W. (2000). *Design paradigms.* Wiley: New York.

Wall, S. & Wall, S. (1995). The evolution (not the death) of strategy. *Organizational Dynamics,* vol. 24, # 2, 6–18.

Walton, T. (2006). Design as a strategy for sustaining loyalty. *Design Management Review,* vol. 17, # 1, 6–9.

Watson, T. (1975). Good design is good business (57–79). In Schutte, *The uneasy coalition: Design in corporate America.*

Wareham, J., Busquets, X., & Austin, R. (2009). Creative, convergent, and social: Prospects for mobile computing. *Journal of Information Technology,* vol. 24, # 2, 139–143

Weick, K. (2003). Organizational design and the Gehry experience. *Journal of Management Inquiry,* vol. 12, # 1, 93–97.

———. (2004). Rethinking organizational design (36–53). In R. Boland & F. Collopy (eds.), *Managing as designing.* Stanford: CA.

Weiner, E. & Brown, A. (2006). *Future think: How to think clearly in a time of change.* Pearson: New Jersey, U.S.

Weinstein, M. (2006). Innovate or die trying. *Training,* vol. 43, # 5, 40–44.

Weiss, L. (2002). Developing tangible strategies. *Design Management Journal,* vol. 13, # 1, 33–38.

Westerman, G., McFarlan, F., & Iansiti, M. (2006). Organization design and effectiveness over the innovation life cycle. *Organization Science,* vol. 17, # 2, 230–241.

Whitbread, D. (2001). *The design manual.* UNSW Press: Sydney, Australia.

Wiles, C. (2003). Take your speech cues from the Actor's trade. *Harvard Management Communication Letter,* July, pp. 3–4.

Wood, N. (2004). Customer value. *Management Services,* vol. 48, # 3, 14–16.

Wu, M. (2006). Corporate social performance, corporate financial performance, and firm size: A meta-analysis. *Journal of American Academy of Business,* vol. 8, # 1, 163–171.

Yetton, P. (2006; Sunday, March 12, 04:04PM). Personal communication via e-mail. (Phil Yetton was co-awarded the Kenneth R. Ernst Award in 2001 by Accenture for "International Thought Leadership," and in 2003, he was recognized by the Academy of Management Journal of Learning for his outstanding contribution to leadership research. He is co-author of the leading text book *Management in Australia*, has written numerous research papers, and is coauthor with Professor Victor Vroom of the internationally acclaimed text *Leadership and Decision Making*.)

Yu, L. (2006). Is creativity a foreign concept? *MIT Sloan Management Review*, vol. 48, # 1, 5.

Zachman, J. (1999). A framework for information systems architecture. *IBM Systems Journal*, vol. 26, # 3, 454–470.

Zaltman, G., Duncan, R., & Holbek, J. (1973). *Innovations and organizations*. Wiley: New York.

Zehir, C., Acar, A., & Tanriverdi, H. (2006). Identifying organizational capabilities as predictors of growth and business performance. *The Business Review*, vol. 5, # 2, 109–116.

Zeiler, W. & Savanovic, P. (2007). Morphological overview in integral building design: Prescriptive reflection. ISADR07: International Association of Societies of Design Research, The Hong Kong Polytechnic University, 12–15 November.

Zimmerman, R., Smith, R., Fernandes, C., Smith T., & Al Darrab, A. (2006). A quest for quality. *Quality Progress*, vol. 39, # 3, 41–46.

INDEX